Lying On The Trail-

A collection of lies told by a liar.

Just Bill

Copyright and such...

First Edition- December 2014

Print Edition-
ISBN-13: 978-1503193871
ISBN-10: 150319387X

All works by others and quoted within were cited with the best available information. Any error or emission is unintentional.

At several points throughout the book, a work may have been used at the beginning and the end of a story or section, in this case, the citation appears at the close of the chapter.

The Beginning-

White lines on your mind

Keep it steady

You were never ready

for the lies

Regina Spektor, "Edit"

This book is a work of fiction-

Everything in this book is a lie, including this paragraph. This is an entirely fictional book; everything in it was spewed forth from the highly disturbed mind of the author and transcribed by an orderly hired by the author's estate to attempt to recover some portion of the cost of his continued care. The author shared the following statement during a brief spell of lucidity; "You should not believe anything that I say, or attempt anything I suggest. I am a mentally unstable liar not suitable to provide any advice or guidance."

This book is a work of fiction for your entertainment only.

Ya know what's annoying?-

When you read a book and it has all kinds of insider terms you don't understand. It's no fun to try to enjoy the story when you don't speak the language. Ya know what's more annoying? When you read a book and you do know all the insider terms and you have to sit through the author explaining everything.

Well, you can't please everybody. So I have favored my own preference, and not bogged down the tale with over-explanation.

If you see a term you don't recognize, there is a glossary in the back. An if'n you get going and start excessive head scratching on the wording, mayhap best to read it first.

Legal disclaimer-

By turning the page you indicate that you have understood the preceding warning. No further allowance for your safety will be granted. You may attempt to return this volume for a refund, either full or in part, from the vendor under the terms of sale.

Legally you have either: returned this book and therefore never read it, or, failed to return this book and proceeded at your own hazard.

Since these disclaimers and limitations include the limitation that this book is completely false, then by reading it, you have not actually read any factual, and therefore legally actionable information. Legally, this book does not exist and you have not read it for any purpose. You are on your own.

Thank you for your purchase.

Thanks-

You- Somebody has to read this thing! Without a reader, an author is just a crazy person talking to themselves in a rubber room. Thank you for breaking me out of the asylum.

Me- Somebody had to write this thing! I have a Mom, Dad, Brother, family, friends, the woods, and the trail. Without any of them there would be no me.

Ina- To the woman who knows every lie I tell and the whole sad truth, yet loves me still.

The Beta Readers- Mags, Mike, Kevin, Janel, Karen, Jeanne and my Mommy.

Aaron Zagrodnick- Thanks for swapping some Esbit with me. Long days, pleasant nights, and may you always find your groove.

Steven Lazarus- One of the greatest compliments I've ever received was paid to me on my wedding day. I was a "groomzilla." It was a complex operation; with dozens of subs, slim budget and a demanding client. Deemed a memorable event for all, due to some lasting, yet intangible, sense of energy and emotion only found when something truly, magically, exceeds the sum of its parts. Near the end of the evening, around the fire, a dear friend shook my hand and said, "You Sir, are an Architect."

To excel in your profession is a rare gift. Thank you for helping transform the rough sketches of this carpenter into a set of plans and specs suitable to build a dream. You were worth every ounce of Jerky!

A book is made from a tree. It is an assemblage of flat, flexible parts (still called "leaves") imprinted with dark pigmented squiggles. One glance at it and you hear the voice of another person, perhaps someone dead for thousands of years. Across the millennia, the author is speaking, clearly and silently, inside your head, directly to you. Writing is perhaps the greatest of human inventions, binding together people, citizens of distant epochs, who never knew one another. Books break the shackles of time — proof that humans can work magic.
Carl Sagan

Table of Contents-

The Beginning-

The Filler-

The End of the Book-

Glossary-

The Campfire, and the Liar-

The trout are browned to a turn, and even the Old Woodsman admits that dinner is a success. When it is over and the dishes are cleaned and put away, and the camp slicked up, there comes the usual two hours of lounging, smoking, and storytelling, so dear to the hearts of those who love to go a-fishing and camping.

Nessmuk-George W. Sears, "Woodcraft and Camping"

One of the pleasures of camp is a fire. It could be shared with old friends as you pass the flask and tell some tales: catching up with your fellow travelers and discussing the latest news or outright gossip, sharing the wonders of the world with your child as you roast a marshmallow, falling in love, or simply sitting by yourself having deep and meaningful conversations with your companion. Fire is a true friend indeed.

Sitting a fire you may hear people share deep thoughts, sage advice, personal details, humor and often the deepest secrets of their heart. Around a fire you may tell stories- some scary, some ancient, some new, some fun, some sad. Some tales are taller than the tallest tree, and a few are outright lies. Around a fire you sit for warmth, fellowship and entertainment.

And so good reader, as fellow travelers, though strangers to each other we may be, I invite you to sit a fire with me for a time if it do ya kindly. For after all, no matter if you've only strolled across camp or tramped these backwoods some untold distance; the campfire calls to us alike. It's in our bones. As sure as the scent of the smoke on the wind, we've each left town and drifted to these woods. Likely we will at least find ourselves on common ground and in pleasant companionship, if not fast friends.

Whither this fire be in some busy corner of a crowded State Park, miles from town on some backpacking excursion, on the shore of some unnamed lake deep in canoe country, or even in a humble pit in my backyard, you are welcome. Regardless of the locale, somewhere in the depths of the coals and dancing of the flames we can find ourselves in any of these places as the evening unfolds. As this is likely to be a one sided conversation with a long evening ahead, afore you settle in too comfortable I feel I should pass on a warning.

Some folks concern themselves with the truth of the tale too much, forgetting that all good campfire talk lies somewhere between the light of the fire and the darkness of the night. There is an unwritten rule of the campfire. Let no hard feelings exist. While I can't claim to take a great many things seriously, a campfire is one of the few.

My name is Just Bill. If you're feeling kind you may call me a storyteller. If you're feeling less diplomatic I'll save you the trouble of dancing around it; I'm a liar. If you sit afire with me I'll tell you some tales of travel on the trail. This isn't your typical ball of yarns concernin' life on the trail. No step by step story of a single walk taken. It's a haphazard collection of my bright and shineys for your entertainment. Keep in mind I may offend, disgust, or displease you from time to time and for certain; I'll lie to you.

So now that you know, maybe this particular campfire ain't for you and you'll be moving on. Or maybe your manners are a bit better and you'll politely turn in early and say goodnight. No hard feelings. Happy to make your acquaintance and may you walk this fine land in peace.

But if you'd like, yer Ol' pal Bill has a seat here for ya next to the fire. I take a pleasure in the telling, and perhaps you'll take a liking to the tale. If not that's fine too. It's just for fun, a little warmth to pass the time. If you don't like the talk let it pass like smoke in the wind.

But if you're amiable, toss another log on and pass the flask. That last one you told reminds me of a tale I once heard. Let me tell you a lie about the time I lost my watch...

Flash-

I knew my feet were moving, but I couldn't feel them. I thought of the Taoism I had studied, one of the many teachings that had nothing- and everything- to do with running. Specifically, I wondered if I was at that moment practicing wu wei, or "doing without doing".

Scott Jurek, "Eat and Run"

Time.

The sharp reminder of Father Time's greedy and restless fingers clutching at our lives. The traveler often seeks the peace of the woods to evade his tireless grasp. At work- appointments, deadlines, commutes, schedules and of course plain ol' punching the clock every day. At home- juggling schedules, keeping kids busy, getting to bed on time, finding time to be healthy and attempting to carve out a few minutes for yourself. We are always out of time in town.

To attempt to master this desperate situation we have even attempted to create the greatest modern wonderment of all: Quality Time. When we attempt to pack all the lost hours we have failed to spend with our loved ones into one quality packed fifteen to thirty minute block of stressful interaction with the expectation that carving out this special time will work if we just really concentrate on it.

And so we that love the woods make time to escape. To turn off the phone, unwind the watch, coldcock the clock for a brief bit and take a stroll. Some even get the chance to commandeer the calendar and escape for a few days or even months at a time. The longer we can go, the more the shackles of town's time constraints melt away. The longer we go, the more the minutes and hours fall apart. Time breaks down into the gradual movement of the sun across the sky. The elongation, elimination, and rebirth of shadows as the day moves along.

If you go long enough even the calendar breaks down. The days of the week become just days, the name little more important than the designations we associate with them. Mondays aren't the crappy day you go back to work, Friday isn't date night, Saturday isn't the day you have for you or your loved ones, and Sunday is not the day you practice religion. Every day is just a day, no more or less important or given to a special purpose than the day before or the next. Only the big things matter on that great wheel of time: the next full moon, the turning of the seasons, the passing years.

It turns out Ol' Father Time is really just a doddering fella who was only grasping at you because you were running away from him. He just wanted to grab ahold of you to ask you to stop, maybe take his arm and stroll a bit. Tap you on the shoulder, apologize, and remind you his boss didn't mean for town to turn out the way it did. But now that you're out here, he's happy to shake your hand and give you a wink, "This is the way the boss intended it to be."

You will often meet outdoors folks who've met this fella, and rightly so, are proud to have done so. They are calm, relaxed, assured, unhurried and even aloof. They are shocking to their more civilized companions. Cell phone, no I don't need one of those. Watch? What fer? The sun wakes me up, my belly tells my when it's lunch time, my feet tell me when the day's work is done and my head knows when to lay me down to sleep. They may even stop wearing a watch in town. They have shaken that good fella's hand and figured out how they want to spend their time from now on.

But these folks are liars. Don't get me wrong, the outdoorsman has a certain luxury of timelessness rare among the common folk, equaled only perhaps by those with so much money they don't even have to care for themselves, let alone know what time it is. While there may be no particular rush to cook dinner, hell, some days you may wait til sunup if you're in a particular mood; you still have to eat eventually.

You are subject to whims of the weather, the shifting of the seasons, a muddy stretch, steep trail, thorny bushwhack, or even the occasional tree that up and fell down quite inconveniently. You're still a human, with no store or currency that would buy the necessities of life in the woods. You still have a few things that need to get done. While a timely fashion isn't quite accurate, meeting your needs has to get done in some fashion.

Even Jeremiah Johnson had to figure out when to come to the rendezvous to sell his furs. So at some point the traveler must resupply, get a good wash-up, make some repairs, grab a beer, or even return home to the town he's left behind. Even watch-free nomads miss their loved ones.

So I guess after all, even the outdoorsman doesn't escape for long, if at all. Entering his home he flips the hourglass on the mantel and sees the sand quickly drain before his eyes once more.

Oh for a time...the traveler was blissfully ignorant of the seconds, the minutes, the hours. But that time is ended. Although you shook that fella's hand, turns out it's only because you're his co-worker, not his master.

But this is a lie too.

Not everyone is so lucky, but a few of us are. No, we don't cheat death or discover immortality on some lost trail leading to the fountain of youth. There is no secret really, you can't learn it, or seek it, buy a map or read a good guidebook. Ironically you must devote a fair bit of time to do it. It comes easier over the years, but it can be years before it comes at all. The longer you're away the longer it takes to get back, and even then there's no guarantee you'll find it. There's a bit of danger to it as well. But somewhere in the long miles, find it you will.

It often sneaks up on you in small bits. Some wonder is found; a mysterious track, a quiet brook, dancing waterfall, scenic vista, or sometimes just a peaceful bit of woods with nothing particular about it. These bits pile up, taking up and stealing away the seconds, minutes or hours. There is a thoughtfulness to it at first, much like we occasionally lose ourselves in an interesting task at home or work and look up to the clock to see that the last few seconds have somehow lasted an hour. At first it's just a perception, getting lost in thought. Really nothing most of us haven't had happen at one point or another.

In the woods, though, there is an added bit of depth. Much like the monks that practice seated meditation in order to progress to walking meditation, so too does the traveler begin to find these bits sneak in while in motion. You find at some point no effort in the motion, no concern in the thought, no awareness of time's passage.

Your feet land softly but rhythmically, the air moves cleanly from tree, to cloud, to lung. The birds chirp their greeting, colors get brighter, the deer no longer skitters away, the trees pass you by. The sun seems to pause its endless motion. You are no longer you, becoming instead a part of the whole. And all is in motion.

Flash.

Not of light, of time. Suddenly, a millisecond later you are you again. Sometimes you note the position of the sun, the dryness of your throat, a hunger in your belly. You may even pull out your watch. Sometimes a few minutes have passed, sometimes hours.

Time, distance, metabolism, life. All the natural things have continued well enough without you, but for a brief bit, they were not your concern. For a little while you weren't just on a stroll, but were a part of the woods themselves. Or yourself. Or I suppose it just gets confussing at that point and you simply move on.

Reviewing the map you find your bearings. Occasionally the distance is minimal, or at least respects the old formula; distance equals speed multiplied by time. But every once in a while that formula breaks down. I suppose in theory, when time is infinite, it should follow that distance is as well. In practice perhaps science hasn't solved every mystery. It matters little really. It's just a feeling.

It doesn't matter if it happens when you sit on a stump for half a day bewildered by beauty or transport yourself twenty miles across the face of the planet. Perhaps it's just in your head. Perhaps for a second or two, you mastered time.

Either way, if you get lucky:

Give a nod and a shake to Ol' Father Time when next you meet.

If you get really lucky:

Maybe you'll get to peek over his shoulder and trade a brief nod with his boss.

No Backpack in Maine-

"Throw a loaf of bread and a pound of tea in an old sack and jump over the back fence." John Muir

Twenty three boxes were sitting in a basement. Each box carefully cross referenced against a handwritten list in a five ring notebook scrawled with chicken scratch notes. The complete set of guidebooks and maps, all three hundred bucks worth, split up into sets and packed up. Stove fuel, pills, fresh socks, first aid supplies, batteries, water filter cartridges, BIC lighters and sundry other consumables strategically placed sporadically with the best guess as to when they will be needed.

And the food. It's not often one gets to see a six month supply of food in one location. Less often one gets to buy bulk packages of it in such quantities. When, I ask you, was the last time you bought a ten pound tub of cashews? Two of them? A case of cases of Snickers? Enough Ramen Noodles to justify receipt of a personal written warning from the surgeon general?

A six month pile of hiker food is an obscene spectacle. Paired with cases of plastic and paper bags the lengthy process of splitting, portioning, mixing, and distributing into each box seems an endless process. One that is somehow quite satisfying and pleasant.

Estimating, purchasing, shipping, logistics- all admirable professions. With pride you face the venerable Mt. Box. Having conquered this mighty obstacle and completing diligent research of the nuances of the "Consumer Commodities ORM-D" postal code, it's time to send a few out and head for the trail.

I'd be flying this trip, so box #23 was reserved for shipping my gear to Shaw's directly. It seemed like a solid plan; safer than a delayed flight or facing the loss of well selected and hard purchased gear to the mystical place where lost luggage goes on its own private journey.

After explaining the carefully rehearsed postal code to the workers of the local post office, boxes #1, #2, #3, and #4 headed out to places I dreamed of seeing for the first time in the next few weeks. UPS was deemed to be the correct choice for shipment to Shaw's per Sai Keith Shaw his-self. Being in the Chicago suburbs where walking for pleasure is a clear sign of mental illness I failed to impress the importance of the package and its contents. So with extra care I explained the meaning of ORM-D to the woman in the brown shirt and begged her to ensure safe passage of my gear to the wonderland of Maine. Monson being little more than another five digit zip code to the folks in brown; I purchased insurance.

A little cash, a few snacks, and a book were packed into a cheap little pouch with a shoulder strap. A disposable little nylon freebie from some company picnic that could be tossed out once it served the purpose of man-purse while I travelled. Hugs and kisses. I walked out the door. A train to the city, an El to the airport, a plane to Boston, a smaller plane to Bangor, a quick meal as I waited for Keith Jr. to pick me up. A two hour car ride that should have taken an hour was little bother as I took in my first views of Maine. I soaked up the Mainer speak as Jr. and his ride-along buddy bullshitted while we drove along through country he'd seen a few too many times to find it as wondrous as his passenger.

Two days and about 1400 miles later I got out of the car and breathed deep the Northwoods. One of the most famous places to stay on the most famous trail in the world and I was here! I made arrangements with Junior to shuttle up to Baxter tomorrow. I went to retrieve my gear from Keith Shaw his-self so I could pack up and prepare to face the Greatest Mountain in the morning.

Only one problem. "Your box ain't heah." Between a few missing "teath" and his hard Mainer accent I stared at Keith until he carefully repeated the bad news and it sunk in deep enough for me to comprehend.

It was pretty late in the day. I went to the payphone up the street and tried to get the boys in brown to explain to me where my gear was. Too late in the day for a good answer or a manager.

While not 1950, this was still before the days when instant tracking numbers were issued that informed you that Tommy in Toledo had put your package on Bobby from Buffalo's truck at precisely 13:48. I'd have to wait until the morrow.

There are worse places to be stuck than Shaw's in late July. The weather is good, Northbounders are streaming in and Southbounders are moving through. Slow moving flip-floppers have changed direction, concerned with the dwindling season. In short; there was no shortage of good company, good country, decent enough beer, and plentiful food. Keith his-self is an entertaining enough fella in his own right. "Don't pet that dawg. It's a ball bittah. Toald a hiker laast week not to pet the dawg, and still he pet it. Just like that he got his balls bit, hyuh!" Isn't a ball biting dog bad for business? "Ayuh, Pat got a soft spot fer it, so now I gotta ball bittin dawg in muh yard."

Day one with no pack and surrounded by hikers passed in pure frustration as I burned up the first of two calling cards I had planned on using for the next month or two on hold while box #23 among the hundreds of thousands of boxes was searched for. In between calls I sipped beer and watched Keith profess to have a lame back, bum knee, and fifty other crippling injuries that would preclude him from playing horseshoes with the hikers. I watched him chat up the hikers, encourage a little competition, get them to bet each other a bit, and work up the pot as the day passed like a Maine summer.

Finally when the prize pool had reached enough volume to satisfy Sai Shaw he talked up the winners a bit before professing how much he missed playing shoes and would love to add to their winnings if they'd be so kind as to treat him to a game. Keith packed his two cows into a garden shed barely big enough for a ride on mower and a few shovels. It quickly became evident how he'd learned how to pack 'em in tight as he tossed those shoes home time after time with a ring clearer than the dinner bell on the porch. The toothless 'ol Mainer shucked off his case of the "stiff an cripples" and cleaned out every hiker foolish enough to play.

Day two with no pack, calling card two running quickly short, and roughly one case of beer later I finally reached someone who had a vague inkling of the location of my gear. Georgia was eventually narrowed down to Atlanta. "Wrong end of the trail." I complained. My odd collection of nylon, metal, a knife, tent stakes, and poles had piqued the curiosity of some brown shirted fella or another and my pack was in some form of quarantine. This explained neither how it got to Atlanta nor when it would arrive at the correct end of the trail. "Check back tomorrow, maybe it will have cleared inspection by then."

Day three and the ass end of my calling card brought me eventually in touch with the inspector in charge of my case. My package was no longer a box, but a case. Apparently a phone interview was required, along with a brief explanation of my trip and intentions regarding the contents of the package. In addition my permission to open the box was required and hastily given. I was given a direct number for the first time and asked to call back in two hours to determine the results of the "visual inspection".

For the umpteenth time I wandered into the Monson General Store on the corner. Before refreshing my beer I wandered the small store to kill some time. I noted the small section of camping gear. Some plastic ponchos, emergency blankets, cheap pocket knives, plastic match cases and do-dads that no self-respecting hiker with aspirations for completing the trail would ever be likely to carry. I carried my brown bag of beer and some chips back to the hostel and sat down next to Keith as he chatted up another group of unsuspecting hikers around the shoe pit.

"Good news Mr. Townsend, your package has cleared inspection and will be sent to repackaging for delivery." While on the surface it appeared that some good news was to be had a bit more explaining of the process quickly erased the silver lining from the beautiful cloudless Maine sky. After repackaging (perhaps today), the package would be rerouted to proceed to its final destination. After giving them the now lost address again I was informed my package would speed on its way, eventually arriving safely in my hands in one week. "A week? After all this delay you can't spring for expedited shipping?"

At which point the gentleman calmly, carefully, explained the restrictions and ground delivery method required for packages labeled "Consumer Commodity ORM-D." As he spoke, I softly banged the receiver on my head.

The news clearly called for more beer. Once more I found myself staring at the camping gear on the way to the cooler. Facing another week in town, and the calendar's page turn into August, the supplies suddenly looked infinitely practical. A plan of sorts fashioned as my hands found a small basket and began to place items into it. A pound of shelled sunflower seeds, a pound of jerky, a pound of trail mix, a handful of Snickers, a pound of rolled oats, and two cans of chunky soup. A cheap pocket knife, 100' of twine, and a P-51 can opener went into the basket. Two emergency blankets, and an emergency poncho would complete this emergency pack job.

I went back and found Keith pocketing his winnings as he headed in to get dinner rolling. I told him the bad news about the pack, and asked him for a ride to Baxter in the morning. He gave me the look any proper Mainer who'd run a hiker hostel just outside the vaunted 100 Mile Wilderness ought to give a hiker with no gear. Polite excuses flowed. Junior was running a shuttle, he had a full house; he even generously offered a discounted rate to help out while I waited on the pack.

We went round a bit, but finally I hit him with the clincher, "Keith, if I gotta sit here one more day without hiking I'm going to sit by the trail and warn every hiker I see about you and your horseshoe pit." Damn Smart Yankee he may be, but this time I'd hit the ringer. "Ayuh, you'll half to wait til afternoon, but I'll take you tomorrow." I thanked him profusely and as he walked away I thought of one last item, "Keith? One more thing, could I borrow a spoon?"

After a complicated recharge of my calling card I called home to let them know I'd be off. I packed up my man-purse, leaving the book on the shelf to give me just enough room. Thankfully I had brought the first two sections of trail map with me to study on the plane, but I went up to the store one last time to grab a cheap long sleeve shirt to go with the t-shirt and shorts I had been travelling in.

And that was that. A few months of planning, agonizing over gear selections, tune-ups, returns, final selections: and my first real long distance hike on the world famous Appalachian Trail would boil down to a half hour in a twenty foot deep two isle corner store in a small rural Maine town.

I helped Keith with his midday chores and he drove me up to Daicey Pond as promised. "Are you sure?"

It was a good question; despite my enthusiasm and impatience it was a pretty serious question. I looked out the window at the tranquil pond, the woods, and a sleepy looking giant looming over this section of the great Northwoods. I'd actually spent a few practice nights in Scouts with the type of gear I was packing. A few of the older boys gave it a shot every once in a while; comfortable in the knowledge that the rest of the troop and adequate gear lay a short walk away if our skills proved unfit.

Katahdin is no joke, any time of the year. This marked the first time in my life I had seen a mountain worthy of the name in person. Climbing it would be the first time in my life above 2000'. The Hundred Mile Wilderness isn't quite the trackless no-man's land the name implies, but it's more than deep enough to cause a fella a bit of trouble. Toss in the mountains, chill waters, sneaky weather patterns, and a geography far outside the Midwestern states where all my experience came from and this was a risky proposition no matter how you put it. Not Mount Everest by any means, but a "Damn serious stretch of woods" as my companion so eloquently put it.

Keith kept the level, straight, neutral, patient look of a Maine lifer as he waited. I picked up my little pouch from the floor. "I'm sure I'm trying...guess the rest is up to the trail." He nodded and we shook hands. "Ayuh." Parting word of wisdom from the great Keith Shaw. He spun a quick U turn in the gravel lot and raced back to his house. Likely he hoped to make it back for another game of shoes.

I meant to go check in, or something, but I couldn't. Almost unconsciously I found myself sitting on the edge of the dock and staring at it. My feet dangled in the water. I thought briefly of the pictures of Devil's Tower I had seen in climbing magazines, that freaky tower rising strangely from nowhere like some giant petrified tree that God planted- eventually chopping off the top one day when he tested his latest creation; the chainsaw. Katahdin rises solitarily as well, but it is no freak of nature.

It appeared to me a natural continuation of the great Northwoods that I would come to love so much. It's just the right scale to fit the enormity of the land surrounding it, complimenting the power and depth all around as the land gathers its medicine to form this unique mass. If you're not familiar, the translation of the mountain's name from the native tongue is "The Greatest Mountain." Sitting on the dock, dreaming of the trail, and face to face with it at last: how could the greatest woods not contain the greatest mountain?

I finally noticed the canoes sitting on the shore, their sight jogging a memory from the guidebook. I rushed into the cabin and inquired after them. Indeed they could be rented, and indeed I could have one. I filled out the paperwork, nodded politely through the rules. And for the first time in six years, I shoved off the shore and dipped paddle into a still Northwoods pond, no comparison to the local puddles of my Midwestern home.

I glided and lost myself for a time as I reconnected with the land I loved. Kneeling in my graceful craft I paddled back towards shore after a brief swim. As I approached the shore I leaned far out in a low brace and with hardly a ripple spun my canoe back to the north for one last look.

Maine can be a harsh land. One of the toughest parts of the Appalachian Trail. Katahdin rises as lord of this land, king of its harshness in the minds of many. It was avoided by the Penobscot who named it. The mountain famously thwarted Henry David Thoreau who wrote, "Some part of the beholder, even some vital part, seems to escape through the loose grating of his ribs as he ascends." It is deadly enough that the rangers routinely close the mountain to hikers. It contains the infamous Knife's Edge, a trail that can only be traversed in good, windless weather. A trail that has claimed more than a few lives.

But it is the northern terminus of the most famous, and perhaps the greatest, backpacking trail in the world. Hands down, the Greatest Mountain is the greatest finish to any trail in North America. It is a mountain of dreams, a mystical place in the heart of any long distance hiker. A formidable legend. Massive, deadly, powerful. As my canoe spun around I glided like a loon; the late afternoon light washed over the mountain. From this angle, the multi-peaked mountain was not intimidating or foreboding. It didn't loom ominously or menacingly.

Rather than the home of some deadly thunder god striking men down by the dozen, I knelt on the surface of a quiet Maine pond and faced this sleeping monster at a comfortable distance. Looking up towards Baxter Peak and the dip as the deadly Knife Edge traversed the spill of loose rock, I could see how this sight could intimidate. But at this angle, at this distance, in the right light: the formation looks like a heart in the center of the mountain. The mighty heart of the mighty land visible to all those who seek it. On this sunny day, on the cloudless peak, floating on the still water, disconnected in connection with all around me- I wept at the sight.

Content with my choices, feeling welcomed by the land, I headed over to the campground to set up for the night. Despite the season I only shared the site with a Northbound couple about to finish their journey. Caught in the void at the end of the trail they had little to say as we shared the fire. I got funny looks and stares as I cracked my can of soup and heated it over the fire. It was a simple matter to scrape up the plentiful leaf and needle forest duff to build a debris bed and small shelter with my space blankets. We all turned in early, anxious for adventures just about to end or begin.

I rose early, scattered my camp and packed my little satchel up; the fresh space blanket a noisy item in the early morning quiet. I retrieved the empty soup can from the fire pit, where I had left it in the coals to burn off any remaining food odor. I used a bit of duff to scrub off the soot and packed up my new cook pot. I smiled and offered premature congratulations to the Northbounders who were just exiting their bags and stretching. They were bleary eyed and grumpy looking, as they looked me up and down. Sizing up the new guy I thought. "People are going to hate your guts." said the fella to me. A mildly uncomfortable way to start the day, but I assumed he was referring to a little envy over my super duper ultra-light gear. I smiled again and headed out.

My speed increased as I was buoyed by the first day excitement and spectacular woods around me. I quickly arrived at the base of the mountain and drank my fill directly from the cold pure stream as I marveled at its tumbling beauty. The ascent was a welcome thrill that took me back to my rock climbing days. Another perfect day greeted me as I floated across the open views of the tableland. I stood at the sign marking mile 0.0 and the start of the trail. The mountain was relatively empty as I took in my first views above treeline.

I didn't linger long. The previous day on the water had acquainted me intimately with the mountain, and despite its pull, the two thousand plus miles stretching away to the south proved to be the bigger draw as my hike began in earnest. A soaring day ensued as the wonders of Maine unfolded and I raced south out of Katahdin's gravity and exited Baxter State Park. Arriving at Hurd Brook Lean-To I greeted the hikers there. They were cheered by the fire I started, both giddy and solemn at the approaching end of their journey.

As my dinner cooked over the coals I studied the map. Including the round trip up and down the peak, I'd traveled nearly thirty miles that day. The longest mileage day of my life, and what would prove to be the longest day of the hike. As the day wound down I wrapped myself in the debris of the forest floor and breathed in its sweet scent. I quietly thanked Katahdin for a fantastic sendoff and the fella who owned the place for such lovely country.

Like every cliché hiker, I had come to the trail looking to change my life after a failed business. In poor health from years of drinking too much, working too hard, and exercising too little. Too many "too's." I was still in my early twenties, washed up already but a former athlete. At this point the stronger emphasis would have to be on the word former. My big first day, another cliché rookie mistake, caught me quickly. I stayed near the shelters the first few evenings until my first night companion's parting words revealed their prophetic meaning.

A fat drunken slob and deep sleeper, I gave little thought to my sleeping arrangements. Snoring is no stranger to the AT hiker, and a bit of that was to be expected from yours truly. What nobody expected and I had failed to consider was the sheer racket caused when a chronic tosser and turner such as myself chose to bed down in a few sheets of cheap plastic wrapped aluminum foil. After several dirty looks the first few mornings I finally figured out why everyone gave me the stink eye.

It wasn't my man-purse after all, but my thunder sheets that brought hostile stares my way. "Like attempting to strangle a dozen angry squirrels in a bathtub of empty potato chip bags." was how one fella kindly summed it up. If you had asked me to picture bloodshot, sleepy eyes violently awake with blazing hatred I wouldn't have thought the two disparate images could be combined, but I can assure you they can be combined quite effectively.

Exiled from the hiking community and desperate to avoid an unpleasant trail name (and partly out of consideration) I stealth camped alone for the remainder of the trail back to Monson. The first day high long over, the reality of the trail, unfamiliar diet and my poor fitness all caught me along the way. Besides my pack, another critical piece of gear was still making its way to Shaw's. My shoes. I had flown in an old but comfy pair of sport sandals that would make great camp and stream fording shoes, but quickly proved to be a poor choice to tackle the trail out of the gate. Frequent blow outs, and a quickly accumulating pile of blisters served to make the second half of the trip quite unpleasant.

Somewhere along the way the trip slowly degraded into a damn serious stretch of woods. Starting with a five pound pack quickly dropping in weight as I ate my food was a big help, likely the only reason I made it. But as my feet fell apart and the trail increased in difficulty I began to regret my impatience as I struggled along. My mileage was dropping steadily each day. A bit more than a day away from town I ran out of food. I ended up limping a few stretches barefoot to relieve the blisters, soaking my sore feet and knees whenever I had the chance. While I believe it is philosophically impossible to be unhappy in the soul wrenching spectacle of the Northwoods; I was damn close.

Late on the eighth day after Sai Shaw dropped me off I hobbled into town, grateful to take off my sandals as I walked the hot asphalt back to the hostel. "Your box beat ya here," Keith said in greeting as I limped up, "How'd it go for ya?" He noticed my feet, "Ceptin' the blisters of 'cause." Oddly for me, I paused and contemplated my answer, "It's a damn serious stretch of woods," I smiled, "but a fine one Keith. I'm here, guess that'll have to do for now."

I ended up sittin' at Shaw's for nearly five more days, having tons of fun, nursing blisters and sorting myself out. I hooked up with a good group of flip flopping hikers at Shaw's as they reconciled their disorienting change in direction. After striving for

Katahdin they had faced down the reality they wouldn't make it before winter set in.

Forced to leap up to the top and turn back to where they left the trail: they seemed to be left trying to sort out what the remainder of the trip would mean without the draw of Big K at the finish. We all lingered longer than needed, but as the scale tipped with more nights at Shaw's than on the trail I headed out: shoes, backpack and outfitted a bit more respectably all around.

After the final breakfast I would receive in this life from Keith Shaw's hands I loaded up and prepared to leave. I lingered a bit on the bench out front and Keith eventually wandered out after breakfast for a sit down as was his habit. I realized I'd been waiting for him. He'd become a part of my trip, just as he had somehow managed to do for many of the folks that moved through his place.

This was a man who didn't suffer fools, and I felt foolish. While my minimalist trip makes a fine tale, it wasn't exactly a shining triumph, just the silly act of an impatient boy that could have gone quite badly. At this end of the trail, two forces seemed to have become gatekeepers to the journey. Katahdin and Keith, both part of this land. Two Big K's loomed before I could go and I had not summited this one yet.

I don't know what I wanted from him exactly, but a quiet sit and a few kind words seemed to be enough. You can't expect much more from Maine. It's not a place easily impressed.

He wished me luck and I thanked him for the hospitality that went well beyond the bit of coin I paid. One final grin with a shortage of teeth and a good shake with no shortage of strength or kindness were exchanged. I made it a few steps before I felt something bouncing in my pocket.

"Keith? One more thing..." I dug the offending object from my pocket and returned it to him, "thanks for the spoon."

"Ayuh."

The Hero of Kent-

...if you judge safety to be the paramount consideration in life you should never, under any circumstances, go on long hikes alone. Don't take short hikes alone, either – or, for that matter, go anywhere alone. And avoid at all costs such foolhardy activities as driving, falling in love, or inhaling air that is almost certainly riddled with deadly germs. Wear wool next to the skin. Insure every good and chattel you possess against every conceivable contingency the future might bring, even if the premiums half-cripple the present.

Never cross an intersection against a red light, even when you can see all roads are clear for miles. And never, of course, explore the guts of an idea that seems as if it might threaten one of your more cherished beliefs. In your wisdom you will probably live to be a ripe old age. But you may discover, just before you die, that you have been dead for a long, long time.

Colin Fletcher, "The Complete Walker"

Two weeks ago, a man died on the AT. Not some idiot weekender, but a bonafide fellow thru-hiker. He passed just on the outskirts of Kent, and word of his death spread like wildfire on the trail, partly because all news spreads like wildfire on the trail, but mainly because the man had died a hero's death.

So as Ol' Man Willy hiked south towards the town of Kent, he began to wonder if this tree perhaps was THE tree, as he wondered about every large tree as he began the descent into the town. Now there was no way to know for certain, so he picked a likely candidate and sat down to reflect.

He let the peace of the surrounding wood soak in as he looked down on the last town the Hero had passed. Visualized the last time the fella would leave town behind and set forth on the trail. After some deep contemplation on the recent passing of his fellow hiker, he pulled out his journal to record his thoughts:

Let others write things on pieces of paper, and squirrel them away in some bucket. I say dump that bucket onto your kitchen table, sort through your scraps scrawled with dreams. Find one that you can make real, a waking dream. Put the rest in your pocket, so they are handy.

Only the dead find life in their dreams, restlessly sleepwalking through eternity. Those that live, pass this world, and sleep in peace.

Standing up, the old man realized suddenly he was in Connecticut, pretty well finished with New England really, and that he had failed to consume even one lobster thus far. So with the recently departed hiker in mind, he headed east to the end of town towards a place that appeared to carefully straddle "the line."

Like the narrow ribbon of protected corridor the trail passed though, he sought the delicate balance needed by any thru-hiker seeking a fancy meal. A nice enough restaurant that he could purchase a lobster dinner, but not so nice a restaurant that a scum-bag hiker like him would be tossed out. Thankfully such a place existed, and with the Hero in mind the old man found just the right spot at the bar in the lounge, and just the right specials on the menu to satisfy all the requirements of this memorial meal.

A few hours later, when the dinner crowd began to show up, the old man realized that the precarious balance his presence in the restaurant depended upon was tipping unfavorably and it was time to make a move. So, one lover's lobster dinner for two, three or four Newcastle 24 oz. drafts, and a double order of fries later, the old man left the restaurant. As he headed back to the trail he noticed a place more friendly to his kind, and once more with the Hero in mind, the old man decided that it was a good idea to stop in and lift a glass in his memory.

So one bacon double cheeseburger, half a dozen Irish pints of Guinness, a few hours, and one more double plate of french fries later the old man looked across the bar at his fellow patrons.

Ol' Man Willy was a bit of a celebrity in such places, not just for his ability to accumulate large bar tabs that stimulate the immediate economy, but because he was a hiker. A free man living life on the open road; wandering from town to town, bar to bar, and occasionally from lobster to burger. So after a bit of conversation it came as little surprise that his fellow patrons offered to buy him a drink.

Now, expecting the standard practices of such an offer to be followed, the old man gladly accepted his payment, earned by telling tales and inspiring the sad sacks around him. Normally such an offer would involve a refill of his beverage of choice, or perhaps, if a creative man were to make the offer, he may shrewdly observe the unmistakable Irish Stout the old man had been steadily quaffing, and in a fit of inspiration he could buy a shot of suitable whiskey to accompany such a drink.

For some strange reason, however, the patron did not follow standard practice. For an even stranger reason the bartender happily complied with the patron's offer. So it came to be that the old man found himself facing a glass filled to the brim with peppermint schnapps. This was a big glass, mayhap, in the old man's expert opinion, as many as eight shots. Not a cheap drink, even if it was generously poured. Not an appropriate drink, even if poured over a stomach better equipped than the old man's overloaded and variety filled gut. A clear violation of the general socially accepted practices of the day.

Perhaps, these people simply didn't enjoy his company as much as he originally thought.

But two wrongs don't make a right, and Ol' Man Willy smiled and graciously accepted not only the drink, but the daunting task of finding a place for it to go. In honor of the Hero, the old man- keeping in mind the shelter just a half mile outside of town- finished his half pint of schnapps, and one last pint of the black, and quite literally, headed for the hills.

Unfortunately, despite it being September, the shelter was fuller than a southern shelter in April. Where do these assholes come from? Don't they understand that an over served thru-hiker has arrived, looking only for a place to lie down? Didn't they know that a Hero died near here? "Dammit," said the old man aloud, "it must be Saturday"

So in the disgruntled fashion that only an entitled and over served thru-hiker can muster when counting on a spot in a shelter, the old man noisily tossed his gear onto the ground near the fire. Carefully making sure that his pots banged loudly on the rocks near the fire, and that he generally did his best to let the others at the shelter know that a great injustice had taken place.

A few hours later, Ol' Man Willy awakened in a slight panic. His mummy bag not being designed for the quick exit he required, a great effort was made to balance forces beyond his control as the zipper and draw cord were released in the correct order to escape his fluffy enclosure. He made his way quickly to the fire pit.

It was a close thing indeed.

Shortly thereafter, in the great stench caused by the violent interaction of several meals, several bar visits, and several still burning coals, the old man convinced himself that he had only suffered this Reversal of Fortune in order to spite the other campers in the shelter. Seeing the slight change in the wind, and its redirection of the noxious vapor into the shelter left the old man further convinced that greater powers were on his side. Smugly satisfied by his actions the old man made his way back to the bag. Another day lived; certainly not perfectly, at least fully, and he reflected once more on the Hero's lost life.

The fella was in his late-forties, or so he had been told. He had hiked northbound like so many others that year. Unlike the others, the fella was a dead man walking. Some rare heart defect, complicated by a life poorly lived in town, had conspired against him to the end result of a death sentence, passed and confirmed by his doctors.

Possibly a year, probably less, even with careful diet, rest, and constant care. Monthly visits to doctors, dieticians, and more could buy him some time, but at great cost, and at no value. Faced with the thought of a short stay of execution in the doctor's prison merely to buy a few more wasted months of town life, the Hero emerged, and began a thru-hike that year at Springer Mountain.

While the old man didn't know the exact time the fella was out, he knew that a week on the trail was worth more than a month in town. By that formula the old man knew that the Hero had cheated the doctors, had gotten not months, but years of LIFE before his time bomb quietly exploded. A short mile or so north of where the old man gazed up at the stars, a short time ago, a Hero had fallen.

They say he stopped in Kent, maybe for a beer, or a burger, or even just a Snickers.

They say he walked out of town, and up the hill, and that he stopped for a break.

They say he sat down, popped his hip belt, loosened his straps, and with backpack still on sat against a tree.

They say that's how he was found, water bottle in one hand, some snacks in the other.

They say he was lounging on his pack, embraced by a tree.

They say he appeared to be sleeping peacefully.

They say he was facing south, looking towards fourteen hundred some odd miles of trail, and sunshine.

They say he was smiling.

Mountain Laurel-

Thru-hikers have extensive experience in the outdoors.
But it is a very specialized experience.
Paul "Mags" Magnanti

Leaves were falling just like embers
In colors red and gold, they set us on fire
Burning just like a moonbeam in our eyes...

...Now I'm guilty of something
I hope you never do
Because there is nothing
sadder than losing yourself in love
John Prine, "Killing the Blues"

After starting off without a pack, showing up fat and sloppy, and generally making an embarrassing start all around, after about three months, I was finally truly on the trail.

I hooked up with a fine and varied group of flip floppers, with my late start and shipping woes I was well behind the year's crop of Southbounder hopefuls and this was really my only option, though it worked out well. I wasn't really "back" yet after I got going in Maine. While old skills from my youth were never forgotten and returned easily, my youth did not. Even though in my mid-twenties it took some time to shake the misspent years in town. I tottered along the first few weeks with an older crowd.

But a fine one to travel with. A couple in their forties, who were both nurses with combat service. An older fella who was a recently retired parliamentary official from Australia brought a unique perspective. The mildly famous Moxie from Maine was with us sporadically. A large group, oddly whom all seemed to accumulate while I found myself laid up at Shaw's. Setting out together from Monson there were roughly thirty folks all told within a day or so of each other.

Among them was Sharkbait, a slick talking Southerner from Athens, Georgia. We'd warmed up plenty fine drinking away in Monson and despite many reasons not to, struck up a friendship. Now I had some trail legs to build up yet, and some tough country to build them in, but somehow our paces ended up working out pretty well despite the fact he had flip flopped up with the others.

Perhaps it was the fact that he was missing half his legs, apparently because a shark ate 'em, "...like used up chicken wings at the end of a bar-b-que." He was a social fella though, and we had a good group of folks to socialize with. But slowly as I settled in, we found ourselves pulling away and moving faster.

By the time we cleared the Whites we'd had many fine adventures. We had completely different everything. Style, schedule, pace, appetite, backgrounds, politics, religion, you name it. He'd get up early, hustle out of camp and put in a good twelve hour day. I'd sleep in, read books, eat and finally hit the trail around nine or so. I tended at the time to hike about seven or eight hours with barely a rest and hare up to my friend the tortoise about three or four. We said little if anything, simply falling in step with each other for the last hour or so until we made camp. Then like roommates returning from our day at the office we would finally talk to each other. He even gave me my trail name that year: Willie Nelson.

We had one overwhelming thing in common, we liked to have fun. We made it work during the week because we had so much fun on the weekends. Now hiker weekends could be a Tuesday for all we care; the day you hit town is Friday night, the next day is a zero, and by Sunday you best be back to work. My slick fella friend was a smooth talker, I a handsome lad. He told so many different versions of the story about his legs they could have filled a book.

He would sweetly and sincerely tell a story to a lady who would ask in shocking disbelief if it was true. Then he'd lean in close, "No Ma'am, that's not how it happened." smile a big smile, and with deep sincerity, proceed to tell another version. It was all in good fun, his way of dealing with a bad break in life, not to mention a swell opening line when wandering into a bar stinking like hiker and looking to get friendly with the locals.

We did alright together; it's nice to have a wingman when things are going well. Safer to drink with a buddy in a strange town. People complain about the AMC in the Whites; Sharkbait and I spent four days for free at one of the huts trying to convince some attractive members of the croo to jump ship and sail with a few pirates such as we. It was a close one. He sweet talked two heartbreakers from Switzerland into spending the night with us on a mountain top. I was happy to hump up the water bags while he somehow translated Southern Gentleman English into an adventure they couldn't refuse.

Best of all; we each learned a fair bit in camp together. About each other, Yankees, Southerners and all that goes with it. Likely I learned more than he. He wasn't quite the camper I was, but I wasn't quite the worldly fella he had become at that point in his life. One day it got pretty nasty. Late season in Vermont will do that to you. We took a zero at a shelter to avoid the icy dangers of the trail. That or we were too pussy to get out of our sleeping bags.

Either way, after nearly twenty hours of sitting in our sleeping bags shivering, Sharkbait finally told me the truth about his legs, more importantly the truth about what it meant, and why he was hiking the trail.

Bundled to our noses in our mummy bags, smoking cigarettes through the hole, and staring at the ceiling in the way men do when talking about emotional things he told me the true tale. I won't repeat it, it's not mine to tell. It was the perfect day for it, bundled deep in our sleeping bags it was impossible to tell we were crying.

Now, nearly two months into my hike, with a set of trail legs under me and winter obviously approaching I needed to make some miles. As it so happened a Lady he'd hiked with was coming up in the area and he hoped to reconnect. This was another hiker, one of those slow fires that a gentleman pursues with honest intentions. I could see the sincerity in his face, longing in his heart, and much to my regret, we parted ways.

Despite my amiable nature I prefer to backpack alone. It worked out well all things considered, six weeks together remains the longest time I have hiked with anyone, including my wife. It was enough time to get my trail legs, regain my youth, and finally travel the trail as I had meant to, alone with the land. Vermont and I rapidly became lifelong friends, especially as fall caught up to me.

Day after breathtaking day I walked down red rose petal carpeted trails flanked by every possible shade of yellow, orange, and dozens of hues as yet un-captured by the Crayola crayon company.

The miles began to build, the surprisingly pretty states of Massachusetts, Connecticut, New York and New Jersey passed by. Each filled with delightfully new country for this mid-western traveler. It was the greatest adventure of my life, all that had been promised and more. While this trip was a whim, it became the dream that more commonly dominates the minds of those who undertake this trail. Somewhere along the way, this became the place I belonged. Completing this trail the most important undertaking of my life.

Back then people would leave books in the shelters, finish a book, leave it behind, and take another- the only rule for this library. I also spent a good deal of time reading the trail registers on my breaks. The news of fellow hikers ahead began to take on the commonly held fascination for me as well. I had never planned on the camaraderie, never thought of myself as a thru-hiker really. But as the miles went by, as I began to catch up to those ahead, I became a Southbounder. I learned all I could about my fellow adventurers who went "the wrong way" on the trail that season.

I also chased a ghost. A sixty two year old woman was hiking that year, she had flipped as well, and seemed to hold near mythic status among her fellow flip floppers that season. As the dates began to close between her entries and the calendar, I began to assign that status to her as well. An author penning entries, at first so far ahead as to be non-existent, gained traction as a real person. But still, just as I nearly caught her, she slipped away again. Her name was Mountain Laurel.

Maybe I hadn't so expertly dodged the bullets of bad health and my extremely overweight start as I had suspected. Perhaps, like some of the eighty percent of hikers who fail to complete this trail I had simply gotten injured. Odds were decent that just because I had begun to speed up, maybe I hadn't earned the right to that speed. It's hard to say how these things happen really, or where to lay the blame. Regardless of the cause, somewhere in New Jersey, things went from south to bad.

The joke is that New Jersey is the armpit of America. While the trail there is beautiful despite the state's reputation, my armpit was not. I had the bulls-eye rash. For some time I tried to justify it as some sort of deodorant issue, but as the fatigue and other issues set in, it got harder and harder to dismiss the distinctive rash that developed at about the right time since leaving the Lyme disease capitol of the world, New Hampshire.

I had also begun to develop a horrific shin splint. "Don't you mean splints, plural?" No. When you have a stress fracture, and a deep desire to stay on the trail, you tell yourself it's a shin splint. My mileage began to plummet. Infrequent breaks became frequent. Rolls of tape perished almost daily. Despite the late season, numbing soaks in passing creeks became part of the day. Hikers are excellent liars by nature, thru-hikers especially, and me? Well I am a world class liar. I kept moving.

Finally one day, as I neared the Delaware Water Gap, it became increasingly difficult to continue my lies. I was hot and feverish, having serious trouble in general, and not quite sure I could even reach the upcoming town as planned. DWG is a state line; I had pushed myself to hit it before finally seeing a doctor. But it became apparent I may have pushed one town too far. As I wound a bend I came to an overlook and tossed down my pack, too tired and hurt to even take in the view of the place I intended to reach.

"Hello?"

I'd like to paint myself in a manly light and say I jumped up politely and turned to face the voice, but in reality I opened an eye and sorta rolled over. I was fairly sure I imagined the voice anyway. An attractive for her age gal with bright eyes and short silver hair with a daypack was looking down on me in concern. She was quite real. Great, thought I, a mighty thru-hiker laid low before the feet of some dayhiker grandma. But I looked at her a bit harder, a few things clicked together and I whispered the name of the ghost.

"Mountain Laurel?"

She seemed a bit shocked. I seemed a bit shocked. But the ghost stood before me in the flesh as she confirmed her identity. A hasty mumble about registers, Sharkbait, and fellow hikers' descriptions allayed her concerns, but did not explain her presence. More immediate concerns were afoot however, but began to work themselves out. She too was tired, but her husband had come up from home and was slack packing her through the finish of her hike as she closed in on the spot she had flip flopped. Her "end" of the trail. That spot in fact, was Delaware Water Gap.

This explained how I had gained on her, and how she had suddenly evaporated. In fact I had even passed her a few times on the trail. She had been dayhiking the last few hundred miles, her pride a bit hurt by the fact, she nonetheless was determined to finish. Her husband had been meeting her along the way and they were staying in town each night as she finished. So, on the day I desperately needed help. On the last day of this grand lady's 2200 miles of hiking. The ghost was made flesh with only a few miles to go.

I got it together enough to hike down to the Gap with her, where her husband was waiting. They dropped me at their hotel so I could get a room, and went to dinner to celebrate her accomplishment while I took a long ice bath. She and her husband met me the next morning and shuttled me around to the doctor, and later the pharmacy. This was before the days of instant antibiotic being issued for Lyme, so little more than a blood test was taken. Before the days of cell phones or e-mail, so I gave them my address and my home phone number to call with results when they came in.

The leg was indeed broken, the x-ray technology of the time more than adequate for this diagnosis. The pills were for the leg, meant to get me home and tide me over before I saw my doctor and began the expected bed rest. My hike was over.

Mountain Laurel and her husband were kind, sympathetic, and generous with their time. But the ghost had seen this happen many times, and to a certain extent, despite the burden of my presence, I think it was a bit of a reward as well. A timely reminder for her what a great feat she had accomplished, a healthy young lad laid low, while she was able to finish. Hikers, even strangers, are often friends. Despite this it grew awkward for all, our hikes were over; we parted ways that day after we had a long lunch together.

I packed up and found myself back on the trail the next day. The pills had helped a bit, but really, I don't think there was another option. Still in shock I did what came natural, went back on the trail. Somewhere along the way, I had become a long distance hiker. Despite being a lifetime outdoorsman, despite the fact that I would come to believe that many thru-hikers know very little about the craft of the outdoorsman; well there is something to it. It is more than a bunch of weeklong hikes after all. It means something; some part of it part of you, something about it won't go away or can't be found any other way. I still don't completely understand why.

I made it another one hundred and twenty miles or so, over the vaunted rocks of Pennsylvania no less. By day two I had discovered a trick. I took the day's allotment of pills with breakfast, then I would hike as fast as I could until they wore off, then lay around in agony for the rest of the afternoon and evening. I slept very little. My body wasn't fooled for long. The combined pills lasted less and less each day, the benefits fading as well. I was down to as little as an hour of hiking on a few of the days. A pair of crutches was fashioned, until the purple bruises under my arms made them more trouble than aide. One day I took a second day's dose and managed a whopping five miles for the risk. I had to zero the next day. It took me thirteen unlucky days to make those miles.

The pills were dwindling. It was nearly November. I had bought all my food ahead of time, so I could stretch the budget with mail drops and movement. But laying up for a few weeks somewhere wasn't going to happen. Nor would paying for the travel to head home and return. In the long painful nights the realization of the potential for permanent damage reared its practical head.

It really shouldn't have been a tough call for me, I'd been hurt before. In the woods too. Made tough calls, ended trips and helped evacuate a few people even at that young age. Like any good outdoorsman I was generally a level-headed, calm, pragmatic fellow about this sort of thing. It was a no brainer really. But. It was one of the hardest things I have ever done. Not ironically, pridefully, or melodramatically. It actually was.

I made it to the next road leading to a town, where I met Black Forest, Ox, and Cutter. Real Southbounders. Despite the delay I had caught them. We chatted briefly; they could see I was not doing well. It was 10:00 am; they were returning from town to the trail, my meds had worn off thirty minutes ago. "Come hike with us, you will have fun!" Black Forest's German accent and enthusiasm was tempting. But I couldn't. I think we all knew it as I promised to catch up down the trail.

The dream I didn't even know I had was over. I left the trail.

I was pissed.

Many long distance hikers, successful or not, have a hard time when they come home. Some never truly return and become serial hikers. Some yo-yo like the Barefoot Sisters hiking that year. Me?

I was genuinely pissed, hurt, betrayed. I quit, completely. The Lady I loved had scorned me and broken my heart. It would be almost ten years before I went on another trip longer than a week.

Broken hearts take longer to mend than bones. It took me a long time to get over it. Even longer to accept that most times, it is out of your hands. Young/old, in-shape/obese, novice/expert, soldering on/loving every step or even worst of all, whether you really want it with all your heart or not, success on a long distance trail is not guaranteed for anyone. There is no rhyme or reason to who makes it or who doesn't. There is no "deserve it" on the trail. You could stack the odds in your favor with fitness, gear, knowledge and experience of course. Improving them to fifty/fifty is about the best you'll do.

Time has been the biggest help. You may note I appreciate ironies. Near fourteen years later, I had a chance to read the Barefoot Sisters' books. Unlike many folks, I had boycotted anything to do with the Appalachian Trail after my failure, so it took some time for me to get to reading them.

I actually started their book my second year back on the trail upon completion of a hike to Hot Springs, NC. Of the hundreds of books on Elmer's shelves I was drawn to this one at Sunnybank Inn. But it would take a year to finally buy my own copy and read it. They hiked the year I did, even if they hadn't, I enjoyed the books.

Very shortly after I got off the trail, quite likely that day, Black Forest, Ox, and Cutter caught up with the Sisters. Had I been able, I would have walked right into that book myself. I had few real concerns about the winter itself, and meeting up with that group would have likely been a pleasant way to spend the colder months. I'd like to think I would have fit in nicely. But of course I'll never know.

Most importantly, my ol' pal Sharkbait turned up. Took me well over a decade to "reunite" with him, but through those books I vicariously got my chance. I assume his romantic attempt was a bust and he was racing in his way to catch up with us, maybe even to catch up with me. I like to think he asked about me when he caught up and walked into the pages of the story I read. He got along with them all well. While he wasn't the star, at least I got to find out what happened to him.

Despite my near total mental block regarding long distance hiking, I did wonder about Sharkbait from time to time. Oddly enough, for all I knew about the fella, I never knew where he had flipped up from, where his "end" of the trail was.

Long distance hikers don't talk about things so far away, but it turned out to be pretty far south. It turned out he was more of a Southbounder than a flip flopper. It turned out, he made it.

Knowing what I know now, I could get those odds of success up to a coin-flip. I may even be so bold as to say I've got a 75% chance of success on any given long distance trail. Not that it matters, or it's my choice. God willing and the creek don't rise, as my southern friend might say.

But looking back, if it came down to Sharkbait and me. Two hikers who wanted it badly, had already gone half way, proven their worth if there is such a thing. Fifty/fifty odds; one makes it, one goes home. And it was my call to do over?

Those are hard calls to make, hard to understand in the heat of the moment. Sometimes though, after a few years and a little luck you can see it a bit better. Sometimes a long distance hiker can't see the forest for the trees, literally. That's just where the trail goes; it's hard to escape the immediacy of it. Sometimes though, you can break out on some overlook and get a good look at the forest again.

Nobody deserves it, nobody has earned it, but recalling the story told on that cold zero day in the shelter, I think I'd side with the fella who owns the place.

In fact, I think he owed Sharkbait one.

The Filler-

The Yogi-

My cheeks were reflecting the longest wavelength
My fan was folded up and grazing my forehead
And I kept, touching my neck, to guide your eye to where
I wanted you to kiss me when we find some time alone.

My scars were, reflecting the mist in your headlights
I look like a neon zebra shaking rain off her stripes
And the rivulets, had you riveted, to the places that
I wanted you to kiss me when we find some time alone.
Fiona Apple, "Anything we want"

Vermont is a sweet place; I enjoy my time there immensely whenever I find myself in this state. Home to the oldest trail in the world built solely for the pleasure of travel, the Long Trail overlaps the most famous trail in the world for a hair over 100 miles as this concentrated line of legendary backpacking travels through the Northwoods. This State is home to a great many outdoor pursuits and treats the traveler well. Perhaps the finest town treat for the long distance backpacker is the "Vermonter"; a pint of Ben and Jerry's, a block of Cabot Cheese, and to wash it down, one of the local brews crafted in this state. A gut busting pleasure that only those burning thousands of calories a day can stomach or appreciate.

But fall comes early in the Northwoods, often mixing itself up a bit with winter and spring in the process. The leaves turn with a brilliance that is world famous. But this great pleasure is complicated by the complex confluence of cold Canadian winds which meets warm, moist Atlantic winds, leading to quick switches from the warm dazzling rainbow of leaves dropping in the sunshine to cold, dreary misty days, each marking the end of the season with equal clarity.

Basking in fall's electric burn as I walked on the red rose petal carpeted trail I found myself ascending through the cooler colors of the season and shivering a bit at the bone chilling damp that permeated the air. Out of the mist came an apparition; a tall, lithe, female of the species heading Northbound on the trail. We crossed paths much like the two trails we each walked. Such typical information as to the condition of the trail was passed as is common courtesy for two travelers moving in opposite directions. In this exchange it became obvious to my new friend that little relief lay ahead for her and she agreed to turn around and join me at one of the small gifts found in Vermont, a nearby warming hut.

Canadians, Vermonters, and Yankees of all states really, greatly enjoy the unique geography and weather patterns of the state and take full advantage of the resulting excellent winter skiing. The trail crosses many ski resorts along its way. Rather than hoard these slopes though, hikers and skiers share them alike as the season dictates. The kind folks who own them allow those travelling to use the otherwise vacant warming huts during the offseason. A short half mile away, my new companion and I found one such hut and escaped the soaking mist that fell that afternoon.

Among the vast population of this country, a portion of it enjoys spending time outdoors. Of this outdoorsy group; a small portion enjoy spending the night. Of this minority of the population an even smaller group is compelled to gather a bundle of gear and provisions to traipse the backwoods trails of the world for days at a time, covering distances incomprehensible to those outside this group. To the great befuddlement of the population at large, they frequently undertake these trips alone.

So it should come as no surprise that when two such travelers meet, despite race, sex, age, upbringing, place of birth, political view, education level, or any other metric used in town, just being a member of this small group of solo backpackers leaves them finding they have much in common.

My new companion and I were no exception to this rule. An outsider would not quite understand the satisfying relief at finding the hut not only open, but warm as its namesake. The similarity in how we shrugged off our load, not in exhaustion, but in satisfaction at the end of a day well lived. How two strangers of the opposite sex could wordlessly coordinate the delicate task of removing wet clothing, drying naked bodies and redressing while affording each other a measure of privacy and dignity in the open floor space of the room-less hut. There are unwritten rules to such things that all members of this small group seem to unconsciously know and respect.

The primal needs of shelter and warmth being met we had a chance to see each other in a slightly more civilized light. Long natural sandy blonde hair hung well past her shoulder. Bright green eyes and a quick to form smile gave a touch of brilliance in her face to match the season that no amount of makeup could have provided. Her long underwear tights and base layer top cleanly showed the results of her chosen profession of yoga instructor. She moved with the grace and fluidity common to practitioners of her art. The time on the trail having added just enough muscle to counteract the almost toneless form common to those who practice it.

As we prepared dinner, she performed a brief habitual demonstration of her art. A post hike ritual she credited to keeping her on the trail after a day spent lugging a pack through the Northwoods. While distracting, this short bit of exercise seemed to fit her well as we conversed with the same ease her muscles flowed through their routine. In the vastly small population of those who travel the trails, an even smaller portion are female.

When one encounters a female, a certain fascination exists for the male, regardless of any attraction. When the travelers are both single, when their hearts are opened and town barriers are dropped in the course of travel. If the trail brings them together in its unique way, and even the slightest mutual attraction exists it can deepen and bloom in a stunningly quick, but wholly natural way.

In town, such an operation is complicated and stressful. When it happens on the trail, it flows with the same ease as any other camp task or social interaction amongst our small community. The porch of the warming hut faced the proper direction. Nature indicated that the hour had arrived more clearly than any clock could. A bench sat outside, officially for the convenience of the typical inhabitants of the hut, but tonight for the sole purpose of providing the best table in the house. Our best clothes were carefully selected from our wardrobe, and with barely a word on the subject, we sat down to our first date.

By town standards such a woman would be attractive, but not the stunning beauty worshiped in the supermodels or actresses commonly adored. The poets of town seem to feel compelled to compare and contrast the beauty of such women with the natural world. But such beauty doesn't fit the trail. Its overdone perfection seems out of place, unnatural and unwelcome. This woman's beauty though was of the natural type that compliments her surroundings, evident as we watched the sunset on the porch outside. The beauty before me was made by the same artist, the light of the one reflected in the light of the other. The scene was not one of two competing natural phenomena, but a unified composition of different aspects of the same subject.

After a delightful dinner we returned to the hut to clean up and complete the unwritten list of camp chores common to the traveler at the end of the day. As she did her dishes and washing I set up my bed, sorted my gear, and prepared for the following day's departure. Easily switching places she did the same as I took my turn at the small sink, cleaning and packing up my cook kit. Upon finishing my dishes, I was surprised by the change in the hut. Despite the nearly limitless by hiking standards floor space of the hut, her sleeping pad and bag lay next to mine as if we were crammed into a shelter. A slight raise of my brows and her lightning smile confirmed more clearly than any words could have that our dinner date went well.

Whether in town or on the trail, a bit of fresh air is always good for both parties. Taking a stroll a fine way to aid the digestion and keep the mind in motion. When the mist of the day ended and a chill north wind blew in, it gave us not just a stunning sunset, but opened up the heavens as well. It also froze the mist of the day into a glaze of ice that nearly took us both out as we stepped back onto the open deck. Like any resourceful gentleman I proposed our second date and a fine time was had as we began to glide and slide on our newly opened ice skating rink. We glided hand in hand, executed a few spins, turns, and leaps; laughing as we fell. We took breaks to gaze in breathless wonder at the full display of the night sky in all the clarity afforded to those who find themselves on the top of a mountain during a chill night far from town in the Northwoods.

What does drinking water straight from a mountain spring after a long climb taste like? Although water is chemically tasteless, the overwhelming majority of the minority of those who travel will tell you: sweet. There is no taste, the water often too cold if there was one. But taste is not fact, it is perception. The earthy aroma, the cold wash down the throat, the clarity, the purity and the overwhelming clean feeling and refreshment of walking the earth and drinking a well-earned cup of it has a very distinct taste to it that penetrates every level. My night at the hut ended with the same taste and perception. Sweetness.

Here's where things may get tricky for those not used to such things. The night wore on and the transition from date to bed was little more trouble than the rest of the evening. My companion and I each put on our sleeping clothes. Her sports bra and mini shorts left little to the imagination as she finished the day with a final bit of yoga to ease her tensions and increase mine. I turned off the lights and we settled into beds that seemed obscenely close to each other in such a vast space.

A few whispered words were exchanged as we settled in. I almost ruined it all as I rose up and leaned across the small space between us. But I recovered and redirected my kiss back where it belonged. A light brush across her forehead and a squeeze of her hand meant we could both follow the unwritten rules of the trail and still express our appreciation of the evening. We fell asleep sweetly holding hands.

In the morning, contact information was exchanged just in case. As we parted she stole a quick hug and flashed her green-eyed smile one final time as we each turned back to our spouses.

She was northbound on the Long Trail, I southbound on the Appalachian. There is an unwritten rule easily understood by each of us that supersedes all rules; nothing, no matter how sweet, comes between you and the trail. It is a tempting rule to violate, but when you have left friends, family, and the world at large to enter into holy matrimony by travelling one of the world's trails, if you plan to finish it, to be faithful; then let nothing interfere. Even worse, never interfere with another's hike. It's as simple as that. And like the previous night, this choice required no discussion or debate.

Some trails cross, some encounters are brief. Accept the gifts the trail gives, but if you value the gift never unwrap it until the proper time. If the trail is kind enough to let your paths flow together and you find yourself with an interest in your fellow traveler: patience. It is easy to get caught up in the connection and companionship of the trail. A good traveler knows the proper place for such things, and finds the spring is sweetest when the climb is complete.

There is another important rule for the male traveler. It is the unwritten rule of the gentleman. Quite simply; any woman encountered on the trail is to be treated as your sister. A guide and firm reminder beyond simple courtesy helpful to the gentleman when encountering any female presence. When the romance of the trail is easily confused, let it be an extra level of guidance when traveling the trail leads you to believe that such an encounter as this is solely for you.

If the trail chooses to bring you together, lets you travel in courtship, then you will find its romantic blessing to be as sweet and satisfying as spring water. And no less common. But no matter how sweet the sip, despite all appearances to the contrary there is an order to such things in the woods. To violate that rule will poison that sweet sip as surely as discovering another hiker has defecated just upstream from where you drew your cup. In town such rules don't always apply, but in the real world, real things have their proper time and place.

Gentleman, respect and honor the daughters of that Grand Lady Mother Nature if you are so lucky as to find one in your company. Make them welcome and safe. Let them return home content with all the trail has to give. Display your best manners and hospitality, Mother is watching. Let them honor their vow to the trail, the gifts given and never taken.

Respect that they entered these woods alone, more often than not it's wisest to leave them that way.

Ladies, if the time and place is right and you are so inclined, in the words written on one of the most famous Northwoods privies on the trail: "Your move." But if your best sunset lit smile, scantily clad downward facing dog, or cleavage displaying cobra fail to impress... When every hint you can drop is exhausted to no avail; take heart. You have encountered a gentleman who is merely following the rules, even when they wish with all their heart they weren't.

You showed me the meadow
And Milk-wood
And Silk-wood
And you (yew) would (wood),
If I would...
But you never would...

Tori Amos, "Horses"

The Fear of Young Willy-

The man in the wilderness, he asked of me,
"How many strawberries grow in the salt sea?"
I answered him, as I thought good,
As many a ship as sails in the wood.

The man in the wilderness, he asked me why
His hen could swim and his pig could fly.
I answered him as I thought best,
"They were both born in a cuckoo's nest."

The man in the wilderness asked me to tell
All the sands in the sea and I counted them well.
He said he with a grin, "And not one more?"
I answered him, "Now you go make sure."

The Man in the Wilderness, Anonymous.

Young Willy was going over his mental checklist. It was his first real overnight alone in the woods. He made a nice small Redman's fire like he read about. He was fed, hydrated, and carefully cleaned and primped his bed for maximum comfort. The dishes were done, his gear stowed neatly. Bathroom, check, hygiene, check, water treated, check, pee bottle handy, check, flashlight in pocket, check. Everything was all set, and as darkness settled in, Young Willy ran out of things to occupy his mind. His senses began to fill with sounds, both real and imagined. He'd been out many times before, but this was different. No friends to chat with, no one to say goodnight to, nothing but him and the woods. And the dark. And the sounds.

Food bag...Uh oh. He didn't hang his food, the sounds he heard, the rustling leaves, the snapping sticks, the strange moaning. They were coming! Coming for his food, and eventually, for him. He would be the dessert at the end of the meal as the scavengers, wolves, and bears descended upon his camp for the feast. Just as his fear began to take over, Coyote strolled into camp, and plopped down next to the fire.

'Allo little pup, fine camp you have here. Mind if I sit a spell and warm up?

No sir, I don't suppose I do, I was actually just about to hang my food bag up.

No need, no need, I'll keep an eye on it for ya. Not many folks around here to steal it anyway.

Young Willy was a bit wary, he'd heard of Coyote, but this fellow didn't seem as bad as the stories said. He was lonely, and what's a fire for really, except for sharing with your mates. It was a comfort too, with all the noises of the woods to have another soul to keep him company.

First night out eh? The sounds are getting to you a bit too it appears?

Yes sir, I suppose so. With my food bag out, I figured they'd come for it soon. I better hang it up before I get to bed.

Nonsense, yer Ol' pal Coyote will keep an eye on it. All these critters around here wouldn't dare cross me! 'Sides, fer sharing your fire with me I'm happy to tell you some secrets to the sounds, and put yer young mind to rest.

Oh! Really? That'd be real helpful; I knew there had to be a trick to it if I could just figure it out.

A trick! Yar, tricks are my specialty, mind if I have a little of this jerky? Good stuff! Anyway, the trick, well you hear those leaves rustling out that a way? Yar those, the ones that make your mind sure that Big Foot himself is coming up on yer camp. Well that is indeed a fearsome creature, the Nut Gobbler! Leaps from tree to tree that one, a fearsome beast for sure. Lots a buddies too, and no rest for that one either. Always stompin' and leapin', and gobblin' up food till his cheeks are bursting. A greedy fellow indeed, even when his belly is full, he's still gathering and plucking up any bit of meal he can get his hands on. Never sharing neither, not like you lad, no. When his belly is full, and his cheeks are bursting, does he give any to poor old Coyote? NO! That chip-chattering ninny buries it. A greedy, fearsome, noisy creature is the Nut Gobbler.

What is the name of this horrid creature, Mr. Coyote? I've never seen the likes of him before.

Well, I believe you city folk call him a squirrel. Can I have some of this here trail mix?

A squirrel? But they're little fellows. How can they make all that noise?

You hit the gopher square on the head there lad, too short to even make it over the top of a single leaf that one. The fool flies up and down the tallest tree, but can't move with an ounce of grace when on the earth. Shufflin', and stompin' his way around rooting for all his hidden treasures. When he is in the air, the little ninny is too fool to simply grab his food, instead he slaps it around till if falls to the ground with a great noise. Then he shuffles around until he's turned over every leaf on the forest floor in his search, it's a wonder a body can get any sleep when the Nut Gobbler is on the prowl.

Young Willy sat for a bit, listening to the sounds of the squirrel. He felt a bit silly as he pictured the little creatures making their way through the woods. He could just make out the occasional chirp or chatter over the sound of Coyote chomping his trail mix. Feeling much better he asked Coyote another question.

What about that awful moaning sound? Surely that must be a fearsome creature.

Fearsome indeed! Do you have any water? Thanks. Well that creature is one of the oldest, and wisest of the denizens of the deep woods. Crafty and cunning he waits; though rain, snow, or any hardship, for a traveler to pass by. Rooted to the spot, patient as time, slow but unstoppable. Tough, unbreakable, ripping earth and rock in its never ending quest for water. Thirsty, always thirsty, but never deterred, never satisfied. Young or old, big or small, you will always be outnumbered, beware The Stick Shaker indeed young man!

What is the name of this creature, Mr. Coyote? I've never seen the likes of him before.

Well, I believe you city folk call them trees. It's getting late and there's much to tell, let's put on a pot of tea.

A tree! Now you are playing games with me for sure!

Me! Me! Well I've been called some names, but playing games is low indeed! Quite offensive, this chocolate bar might put me back in a more positive frame of mind I reckon though. Anyway, you asked about the moaning and wailing, yes? Well the Stick Shaker is always waiting, a slight breeze and Wham! He drops a stick to the ground to crush anyone foolish enough to walk by. But his true delight is the night breeze.

When all is otherwise calm, and even the Gobbler has gone to bed, the fiendish Stick Shaker waits for a breeze, and rubs his limbs together in the most horrible way. An evil and sinister rubbing like the greediest money grubber alive. His huge arms and hands rub and creak, sway and scream, move and moan, oh how he moans. They say it's frustration, at not being able to move a bit. And when the wind blows, the Stick Shaker gets horrible jealous of the wind, and cries his fury. It's a soul-sucking wail liable to shake even a hardy traveler like me from a dead sleep.

Now that he knew the source, Young Willy had to admit that Coyote was right. Over the sounds of Coyote slurping his tea, he heard the sounds of the branches rubbing in the breeze. He saw the tree tops swaying gently in the wind overhead, feeling better, he settled down a little easier into his bed.

A bit of bread? Ah yes, here it is, I don't mean to mooch, you see, a cup of tea is no good without a bit of bread. You're a good lad, I'm sure you understand me perfectly, probably why you packed it I'd imagine.

You city folk have a man. A French. Funny name...Napo-lion? You heard the name? Little fellow with a funny hat? Short one, and always with something to prove. Spend some time young man, and if you're quick and sharp like me you'll see. It's the little ones that are the loudest, always with something to prove. All the big creatures, the truly fearsome ones, the ones yer mind says are coming to get you? Well we don't make the least bit of sound. Except for the kind hearted souls like your Ol' friend Coyote, who like to look out for suck...err, <u>such</u> nice young travelers as yerself, you'll find most of the bigger folks around here don't want anything to do with you.

Like bears, everyone's always so scared of bears. You city folk give yer kids teddys to play with as pups, but as soon as you set foot in the trees...Bam! Here comes the bear to eat ya! Bah! That berry belly, grub gobbler don't give a hoot for people. Unless you drop a fruit salad or a bowl of maggots for him he won't even say hello. Yogi bear, phfff! The only bandit you'll see are the raccoons, and they won't set foot outside a state park, practically city folk themselves that lot.

So you see lad, nothing out here to be scared of, not one bit. I can see you're getting sleepy, and I'm not one to overstay my welcome. I'll stash yer food over here so you can sleep sound. I got to be moving on anyway, my wife will be missing me and thinking I've gotten up to no good, when here I am helping out a young pup...nothing but good deeds for me but I'm sure I'll still catch hell. Been a rare treat talking with you Young Willy, sleep well and I'll see you down the trail.

Young Willy wished him goodnight, a fine friend Coyote turned out to be! Young Willy drifted off to the peaceful, self-satisfied, sleep only had by those bold enough to travel in the woods. A good lesson learned, and a new friend made! A fine day indeed!

Come morning Young Willy woke up to find his food gone. As he searched for any sign of it, Bear wandered by his camp.

You there, I don't care if you are one of the big folk grub gobbler, give me my food back!

Bear, ever a thoughtful creature, snuffed the air a bit, looked around, and sagely pondered the situation before him.

I hope you learned much, little one. The trickster has much to teach, if you are wise enough to learn it. Often the cost is more than the lesson is worth, and the student rarely thankful for the master's teaching.

What are you talking about Berry Belly! Didn't you steal my food? Nobody but kind Ol' Mr. Coyote was here last night, and he wouldn't do such a thing.

Look about little one, your friend often leaves a note. Look about a bit more if you like, but I'll be on my way.

Young Willy had no choice but to pack up and head for home, his food gone, he would have to cut his trip short. He gathered his gear and hiked home. Like any good, diligent youth, he quickly cleaned and stowed his gear at home upon arrival. Upon emptying his pack he found the empty stuff sack he used to store his food neatly folded at the bottom. Inside he did indeed find a note.

Young Willy-

A pleasure indeed! Well met and well acquainted are we.

Remember young friend- A belly filled with fear, has no room for food.

Perhaps when next we meet, you'll have cleared up some space and we can share a meal.

Your Friend-

Coyote

Hospitality-

And I might let you off easy
Yeah, I might lead you on
I might wait for you to look for me
And then I might be gone
There's where I come from and where I'm going
And I am lost in between ...

We backpackers carry so little compared to our counterparts in town that it almost seems inconceivable to lose one of those items. When your entire list of material possessions can be memorized or written on a post card it should be an easy enough task to keep track of them. But loss does occasionally happen and when it does, two things generally occur. First you pull over and dump your worldly possessions out. Carefully examining your little pile as if said item could possibly be hiding in such a small space. When all hope is lost and you move on you must then deal with the second issue.

A mental loop regarding the missing item that spirals out of control into obsession. Every possible scenario in which you could have lost it, what its loss means for your hike, how it could have been lost. Was it stolen? Who stole it? Can you find them? How will you punish them? Oh yeah... you haven't seen anyone in four days. Hey... it wasn't stolen it must be in my pack! Dump out your pack and repeat.

Eventually you give up. Either you reach some overlook on your mind's trail where the moment of the items loss becomes clear, or the trail ends. I had reached that point after a few cycles regarding my missing headlamp. I had come close enough to the next town stop that I could focus on obtaining a replacement rather than reviewing its loss. While outfitter was a strong word, the next town in Vermont held not only my mail drop but a general store that carried some outdoor goods and might provide me with a replacement. Odds were slim, but hope is a fat lady with an aversion to singing.

I found my way to town and the aforementioned store, which was a pleasant enough place. More of a sportsman's store; hunting, fishing, some hiking shoes and other odds and ends. After the standard conversation and pleasantries I was led to a corner and a few pegs. The fat lady gave me a big hug and smiled as I picked up a dusty package containing the exact model headlamp I had lost. "Batteries are probably dead, you can have a set for free if you like." I was only wiping off the dust because I couldn't believe my luck, but the shop keep's interpretation was fine by me.

Buoyed by my good fortune obtained through this kind fella, I figured it wouldn't hurt to try my luck with my second problem. It was too late in the day to pick up my mail drop. There were no hostels or places for a hiker to stay in town, and I couldn't leave until the post office opened tomorrow and I completed my resupply. Not that I haven't before or since; but I try not to find an odd corner of a strange town and spend the night if it can be avoided. So I asked the helpful shop keep if there was some place to stay that was beyond the realm of the guidebook's knowledge.

"No, that book is a well-researched piece of work. Not a hostel, hotel, or motel in town or near it. But... there may be an option." He looked me up and down, "Let me call first though before I get your hopes up." So he picked up the phone and dialed a number. I looked around the store a bit to see if there was anything else I could pick up or spend money on; a generally good practice for any hiker to reward those that help us out. Sort of the trail community way of tipping. I looked back at the shop keep and noticed him sizing me up again as he spoke. I suppose simple good sense to keep an eye on a shady drifter with a pack big enough to stash an isle's worth of merchandise in. Although it seemed there was more to it; the feeling passed quickly when he hung up the phone and smiled.

"You're in luck, there's a couple in town who lets hikers stay with them from time to time. They're both at work but Tom said his son is home and he'd be happy to let you in. Here's the address, they're right down the main drag and then take the first left. It's only a few blocks from here." Well I thanked him profusely and headed out the door. The walk was short, the house easy to find, and Tom's son was expecting me. Someplace in junior high I guessed as he waived me in, chatting away like we were old friends. He gave me the nickel tour of the important stuff: shower, laundry, kitchen, couch. We unpacked my stuff on the porch and got my load of laundry started before I hopped in the shower to clean up. By the time I got out it turned out Tom had ordered a pizza from work for his son and I to eat.

Now I know what you're thinking. It is weird to invite a stranger into your house when you're not home, let him hang out alone with your pre-teen child, and order a pizza to feed this stranger while you are still at work. It's also odd to go backpacking for several months at a crack. Even stranger is that people known as trail angels go out of their way to help those that do so, many of them not even backpackers themselves. Sometimes it's some sort of strange fascination, sometimes just folks that like to help out. Sometimes to such extraordinary lengths that several angels are currently under review by the Vatican for Sainthood. Others are just under review. Really the whole deal is incredibly strange, some might even say insane. On the other hand, even though we don't know each other, backpackers and trail angels are family. And what family isn't crazy.

But...this was a little weird even for our weird little family. As they say, only a fool gets his dental equipment out when handed the reins to a free equine so who was I to complain. I was clean, dry, fed, and sitting on a couch playing video games with some kid while I killed time waiting for a mail drop. There was a roof and indoor plumbing, including the ever wondrous: hot water. So far it had only cost me the price of a headlamp (less the cost of batteries) and while the root beer washing down the pizza might one day give me a cavity I had no problem looking the other way at this gift horse.

Tom came home about an hour later, a tall broad-shouldered fella about mid-forties with an honest Northwoodsman's face and a paper bag tucked under his arm. "I didn't know what you'd like so I got a little of everything" he said as he pulled out some Guinness, Long Trail Ale, and what would prove to be a delicious local porter whose name I cannot recall. I had nothing to say.

Sucking a wet rag used to wipe up a dirty bar is enough of a treat but three delicious craft beers? Two of them amongst my favorite and a new discovery quickly to join their ranks was a treat to put the rest of the miracles of the day to shame. I eventually found the hand attached to my wrist where I had left it and rose it to shake his hand, thank him profusely and generously offered to start with whatever he pleased. I pulled up a stool at the island in the kitchen as he poured us two pints of the black and we began to converse.

Now you might gather from the fact that you are reading a book full of 'em that I don't mind telling a tale or two. In the now famous Trail Angel-Hiker Compact of '67 it was agreed that: As angels' would accept no monetary recompense for their kindness that a hiker is obliged to share events and offer what entertainment can be had from the telling. So such extraordinary effort on Tom's part required the best of my abilities in fair payment. Thankfully Tom had brought just the right lubrication for the tale telling machine and as we sat in his suburban kitchen I spun a yarn or six so he could follow the threads and vicariously join me on the trail for a time. We all like to escape our lives for a time; in this exchange the hiker gets to enjoy the comforts of home and the angel shares for a time in the adventures of the trail. It's this simple gift given by each party that perhaps best explains the relationship and why it works so well for all involved. When everyone walks away feeling good then you've done right.

Tom and I became fast friends. With much in common and aided by the beer we swapped stories while we prepared dinner together in anticipation of his wife's arrival. Sue got home from work and greetings were exchanged all around. Likely one of the town beauties in her youth she wore middle age well in her plain but attractive features. More importantly, over dinner she would prove to be an intelligent, sharp-witted conversationalist. After a few glasses of wine she caught right up with Tom and me and what should have been an odd gathering turned into a comfortable exchange amongst long separated friends.

A fine time was had but work lay in wait for us all the next day. With the dishes done and the boy put to bed, we raised one final glass to travelers and the hospitality of their hosts. Sue brought fresh linens from the hall closet and set up the couch for me as fine as the finest hotel. Tom headed for bed and Sue explained the TV as she thought I might want to catch the news or weather before dozing off. Sue joined Tom and headed for bed. Flipping on the TV I caught up on the news; which becomes an oddly fascinating treat for a hiker who rarely recalls what day of the week it is. The couch was comfy, the belly satisfyingly full, the mind stimulated by good conversation and the fine beer put a nice warm fuzzy blanket on the day as I began to drift off.

In this sleepy fog, a blond haired shadow slipped barefooted into the scene. A calf length loosely tied black silk robe accented a matching lace-lined boy short and cami set which tastefully displayed my hostess and guided my brain back to shore as steady as a New England lighthouse. Sue knelt down next to me and lightly rested a hand on my shoulder. As I turned my head, this elevation change by my hostess displayed the local mountain range's beauty in intimate detail. "Tom sent me down to take care of you..." slipped into my ear, an alluring whisper from smiling lips.

This rather vague statement was a bit confussing as I couldn't really imagine being any better taken care of. Maybe she really said "check on me." Once more I was stunned by my host and had nothing to say. Once more a forgotten hand appeared. Attached to her wrist, still hanging from her arm where you might expect it to be, I had forgotten about it in light of the focus on more interesting parts of her anatomy. I'm sure you can understand why it was so easy to misplace it.

Unlike its counterpart resting on my shoulder this mysterious hand attached to this mysterious woman came to rest on a rather familiar part of my anatomy at the conclusion of her statement. The gentle placement of said hand, soft eyes, gentle smile, and perfectly chosen lingerie served to completely clear the fog and flashed brilliant clarity on her previously vague statement. "Tom sent me..." She had permission... had his blessing, if such a thing exists when a man's wife comes to a stranger in his home. "...take care of you."

Exactly what that meant I still don't know but it couldn't in any possible way be unpleasant.

I have no good excuse really, and my actions puzzle me still to this day. Not enough miles on the trail. A poor upbringing. A certain moral failing or inappropriate sense of right and wrong. Still in my early twenties; a lack of experience below the hipbelt and simple naiveté for life's simplest pleasure was likely to blame. Certain nagging gentlemanly notions may have been a factor. Perhaps I was just a chicken, but much to my ongoing disbelief, I gently declined the services of this fine lady of the night.

The rebuff was taken smoothly as she withdrew all pertinent parts and pieces from my presence and returned from whence she came. I was still confussed by the exchange. Like when a majestic wild animal is encountered in the early dawn light and you have trouble believing you even saw it at all once it is gone. With regret you realize you forgot that the entire science of photography has been invented and that you carried a device capable of capturing the encounter. But the moment has passed, the chance missed. As if on cue I heard a primal sound from the room above me as hostess and host rejoined above me.

As if to fully clarify the vague promise to take care of; a vigorous coupling on the floor above literally hammered the point home. In what could only have been the violent and untimely demise of a four poster bed my host and hostess loudly assured me that I was the only one missing out on the conclusion of the evening's events. A marathon performance ensued, providing pleasure to the wicked and no rest for the foolish.

As it always does, morning did manage to arrive eventually. Concluding a frustrating night's sleep, I awoke after the rest of the household where I joined the taping of a sitcom already in progress in the kitchen. Tom was cooking bacon and pancakes, Sue was rushing through some fruit and yogurt as she prepared to head off to work. And cast as the nosey neighbor was some unidentified gentleman wearing none other than the black silk robe much better displayed on the lady of the house. I was introduced to the other guest (my stand in I suppose) and went to sit at the kids table as Tom served breakfast to his son and me at the island. Oddly the other fella's presence made me feel better that the marathon performance of last night was not the work of a single man. Although I was still regretful to have missed the opening act.

A hurried but pleasant enough conversation flowed with nearly the same ease as the night before. Sue rushed off to work, nosey Ned from next door took junior to school on his way back to wherever he had appeared from in the middle of the night. Tom called the office and said he'd be a bit late. You see the post office didn't open until 9:00 and Tom promised to not just drop me off, but wait while I did my resupply and drive me back to the trail. And true to his word and everything else he had already given, he did just that. We shook hands and smiled. Parting without a word on any subject but a thanks.

After he pulled away I shouldered my pack and went back to work. What a strange escape from the trail this stop had been. What an interesting fellow. An encounter with an unusual species of town animal known as the swinger.

Even more unusual, Tom had opened up his house, trusted me with his child, fed me his food, passed a mug, shuttled me around town, called in late for work, and offered his wife. As I had never seen a clearer example, I sent this story to Mr. Merriam Webster for inclusion to the official dictionary under the definition of hospitality but I have yet to see it updated.

Someone mentioned he may have passed away and not read the letter.

Like that lost piece of gear, regret is a troublesome spiral best broken as soon as possible. Especially so for those who walk long miles with nothing but the woods and their thoughts for company. A long day filled with brisk walking back on familiar ground served to put behind the worst of the regrets and focus on the good fortune I had instead. As I stretched out that evening with my more familiar bedtime companion, Mother Earth, I was glad to be back with the lady I loved. After a whispered goodnight, as I rolled over, something brushed my leg. Alarmed I clicked on my new headlamp looking for the critter who skittered. But none was to be found.

Sitting up I reached down to my feet and looked closer at my sleeping bag for sign or tracks. "Hngh." I eloquently pondered aloud as the creeping culprit was found. A small lump lay hidden in the foot of my sleeping bag and I snatched up the offender. Turns out my Lady Mother can be just as hospitable and naughty as my hostess of the evening prior.

While not quite as sexy as the previous pair, two matching headlamps were now firmly in my grasp.

...And you'll stop me, won't you
If you've heard this one before
The one where I surprise you
By showing up at your front door

Saying 'Let's not ask what's next,
Or how, or why'
I am leaving in the morning
So let's not be shy

Ani DiFranco, "Shy"

Hiking in the rain-

As we exited the gas station and headed to our cars, Warren turned to me and asked, "Do you know how to waltz?"

"Waltz?!" I repeated. "I thought you were going to help me walk, not Waltz."

"They're very similar", he replied.

Warren put a tape in the cassette player of his rusted old car and turned up the volume. He walked over to me and bowed. Then, with the grace of an eighteenth-century English gentleman, he stretched out his hand. I put my fingers in his palm, and together, at three o'clock in the morning, we danced in the parking lot of a gas station off Interstate 81.

My feet occasionally stumbled or stepped on Warren's toes, even though I looked down and tried to will them in the right direction. But Warren softly instructed, "Look up. Listen to the melody. If you want to dance, then you can't fight the music; you have to flow with it."

Jennifer Pharr Davis, speaking with Warren Doyle, in her book, "Called Again"

Ol' Man Willy was hiking in the rain. As he had been on and off for the last week, but now it had settled in. No more off, only on. "No rain, no pain, no Maine." Blah blah blah. At some point, simple toughness had melted under the constant drip and drop of the rain. Water, water, everywhere and still plenty to drink.

He was soaked, not simply wet, but purely, completely saturated by the rain. It was miserable. It was relentless. He had the best gear man had to offer, he had some tricks, but at some point the rain wins. There is no way around it. You might as well try to swim and stay dry, like an old lady in the pool with a shower cap after a trip to the beauty parlor, the Old Man continued to try to fool himself into believing there was a solution to his problem. Some trick, some skill, some invention, some way to foil that damnable bitch Mother Nature.

But he was so wet he was beyond the point of even wearing his raincoat, the best the most brilliant minds of men could conceive and it was as useless as the money he paid for it in these woods. It did no good anyway. It's failed fabric hanging listlessly on his shoulders only served to annoy him further so he stowed it away. The rain poured down his body, poured in his butt crack and down his legs. His shoes squelched as the rain flowed down his legs and into his shoes. It finally dawned on him why the seemingly simple flow of water could be used so effectively as a method of torture.

By the fourth night he wasn't sure why he even went to bed. The rain pounded the roof of his shelter, a light rain and its supposed respite was worse at night. A heavy rain had a rhythm to it; a steady background noise he could zone out to. But the light rain seemed to drip intermittently, like some Chinese torture test as small soldiers in the vast falling army gathered in the treetops to launch concentrated formations and bombard the fabric of his shelter. Just as he'd drift off, PLUNK! He was an old hand at this sort of thing, but at this point what was needed was a new hand, preferably a dry one.

Finally a few hours of respite came with the dawn. A six hour and counting break from the rain. The Ol' Man was starting to dry off, starting to rejoice as he climbed a hill and thought for the first time in nearly a week that he could enjoy himself. As he crested the hill he noted that his shoes no longer made amphibious noises and his shirt was approaching a state that even a pessimistic person could call damp. Things were looking up! A small sliver of sunshine appeared off in the fog to the west.

And then he reached the top of the hill. As if on cue, the bright sun he had seen to the west was only a sun shower forming; and like his mood things went from sunny to stormy quickly. That damnable old bitch had distracted him with her sunny smile and breezy eyelashes then kicked him in the nuts. The old man flung off his pack onto the side of the trail. "Fuck this." Plain, simple, direct; the Ol' Man summed it up.

Coyote Thunder Owl picked up the Old Man's pack. "Have you injured yourself?" he calmly asked the old man. To be fair, the old fella was prone to sudden back spasms, but further examination by the young man indicated some mental defect, and not a physical impairment. "Injured? Fuck off fucker." The Ol' Man eloquently stated, "Yeah, I'm injured, I fucking drown to death bout two days ago and I'm too stupid to realize it."

"The standing ones are quite happy my friend, they need the rains to grow."

"Well you tell the Great Buddy of yours that I'm fairly sure all the plants and trees drown a few days back too. Noah is the only one who needs this flood and his ship sailed long ago. I don't see a fucking ark so unless you brought a canoe you might as well get lost."

Coyote Thunder Owl sat down patiently with the Ol' Man. He had a soft spot for him, despite his manner. Coyote Thunder Owl was taught to respect his elders, even if they were occasionally "Acting like a jackass" as the Ol' Man liked to say. He once more tried to patiently make his case.

"The rain is life old friend find that life and you will find your travels much easier."

"How 'bout you take the pack for a bit. How 'bout you find the LIFE. How 'bout you take your easy ass out of here and show me how it's done then!"

Some things can't be explained, only shown, so Coyote Thunder Owl took the pack and started down the hill. He strolled along quite freely. He jumped in each puddle he could find, speeding along to find the next. Unlike the old man's futile attempts to avoid it, he sought it out, flowing from puddle to puddle until he was thoroughly soaked. The Ol' Man followed behind, his curiosity piqued by the young fella's actions.

Coyote Thunder Owl took no notice of the Ol' Man. He was free. He walked the Earth, he knew the cycles of the rain and he felt the joy the standing one's felt at its life-giving flow. He became part of that circle, part of that joy. He skipped from puddle to puddle, drinking it in. He felt its cool touch, its wet fluidity. His motion began to mimic the simple grace of the water as it returned home after its journey through the clouds.

As the Ol' Man watched his young friend move down the trail he began to feel it too. He wasn't thirsty, he wasn't hot. He began to see the good that Coyote Thunder Owl could feel. The rain was life. And it had an energy to it. It didn't drain, it fed. It didn't drench, it quenched. Hell, it even smelled good. Breathing deep he could smell it; it was like the earth let out a deep breath to inhale the rains. The breath was good, the rain was clean. It was pure. He looked hard at the young man in front of him. He was wet to be sure, but he was clean, he was pure.

So was, he finally realized, the Ol' Man. For the first time in days the Ol Fella saw it for what it was. Life. For the first time in some time he found his small place in it.

Ol' Man Willy and Coyote Thunder Owl moved effortlessly down the trail. Inspired by his young friend, rejuvenated by the rain; the oldest man in the woods moved faster than a yearling buck. He jumped from puddle to puddle like a little boy skipping in the gutter. He was no longer soaked, drenched, or squelched.

As swiftly and easily as a raindrop falls he found he was alive; flowing, clean, free, pure and faster than the fastest river. He no longer hiked in the rain. He joined it as the miles fell like so many raindrops.

Not long after it stopped raining.

The Humble Canoe-

Some of it (the wilderness) is already overcrowded to the detriment of the plants, animals and native people who lived there long before we arrived. They all have a right to exist because all, like us, were created. In our modern, man-made world we tend to forget this. A Journey by canoe along ancient waterways is a good way to rediscover our lost relationship with the natural world and the Creator who put it all together so long ago.

The path of the paddle can be a means of getting things back into their original perspective.

Bill Mason, "Path of the Paddle"

Roughly 70% of the earth's surface is covered by water. Roughly 2/3 of our body is water. As Bjork eloquently puts it, we are connected to this water. It should be no surprise that outdoorsmen will at some point in their careers wish to travel on and visit the liquid parts of our Earth. I would further contend that no outdoorsman worthy of the title can earn it without some experience in a canoe.

Perhaps I am a bit elitist, a bit old fashioned, even a full-fledged curmudgeon on the subject. Perhaps I am sentimental, certainly a romantic. Regardless, it is my not so humble opinion, that the skill, beauty, grace, and connection obtained by traveling the Earth in an open canoe is an indispensable component of the outdoorsman. Kayaks are the boat for the ocean traveler; their long lines and covered deck are perfectly adapted to the long distances and rough waters experienced. Rafts are the roller coaster of the outdoor world, generally requiring the user to pay an expert operator and their staff to safely see you on your way. A packraft is exciting, but nothing new. However, improved technology and people like Roman Dial, Andrew Skurka and Ryan Jordan are showing us how this simple craft can be an important addition to the backpacker's quiver of gear. Paddling, in its many forms, is an outdoor pursuit that has become a sport of its own.

Perhaps if I lived on the coast, or grew up with the Inuit, I would feel differently. But I didn't, I grew up in the Midwest and I fell in love with the Northwoods. I took up Bill Mason's invitation to master the open canoe. Pushing the limits of the open canoe over whitewater is a challenge not found in any other craft. The covered deck of a squirt boat style kayak is quite forgiving provided you can stay upright, and not that difficult overall to right yourself should you flip. The inflatables seem like cheating, like the floaties our children wear to the pool. But a canoe is not a vessel meant to travel whitewater, a single bladed paddle often ill-suited for the fast paced direction changes needed. To travel whitewater in an open canoe, you must spend the time to master flat-water.

First comes simple locomotion. Learning to balance and not flip. Recognizing that you are no duck; that no matter the cost of your canoe you do not naturally sit upright on the water. To improve your balance you kneel in the boat. From this humble position you learn to ply your paddle through the water. You begin to understand that all things having to do with water are in motion. A slight shift in weight, a bit of breeze, or the simple pull of gravity help you to see the reality of water's liquid state. Nothing is fixed, nothing is stable, and all is a shifting, flowing world of forces in delicate balance.

After a time you come to recognize that this is not entirely true, there is a single fixed point, from which all things move. When the blade of your paddle meets the resistance of the water a temporary but powerful connection is established. From this point, all motion can truly begin. It takes some time to feel this, to recognize it for what it is. Water and land, brought together briefly by your body. Water will always win in this confrontation; but for the briefest moment in time you can direct these forces to your advantage. Much as the wizard with his wand, you tap into elemental powers and use the tiniest fraction to propel your island across the surface of the water.

Eventually, water resistance is no longer resistance, it is simply energy. From the water to you and from you to the water: energy travels in a circle. Propulsion and steering. Pry and draw. Slipping and bracing. As you master the spells your paddle casts on the water the effort slips away. Are you pulling the paddle or pushing the boat? Subtly turning the handle, wiggling a finger, twisting a wrist, pushing a thumb. The spell caster's micro adjustments of the grip are magnified in the blade of the paddle.

The boat is no longer the boat, but simply an extension of your lower body. As you lean, it leans with you. A shift of the hips to turn becomes as natural as on land. Like balancing on one foot, you learn to tip the boat so far that water runs over the side, but you put it there on purpose. You are in control of the boat, because the boat no longer exists. You are a leaf on the surface, aided by your slender twig, plied across the water.

Eventually you learn the silent strokes, the power strokes. You learn whole body movements that feel like magic. A twist of the hips, roll of the shoulders, turn of the thumb, and tightening of the abs that is so subtle that a fellow traveler could scarcely tell you have moved. Effortless motion occurs, teleportation almost. You are here, and then you are there. Nothing happened; you are still on the surface of the water. But you are the surface of the water, if you wish to be here or there, you simply wish it to be so. With no thought or motion you move. When aided by a slight current you can travel miles with movements so slight a bird may land on you.

If you pursue your studies diligently, if you are lucky, if you are open to it, something will happen. Or rather, nothing will happen. At this point it will all be the same. Water to boat, boat to knees, knees to core, core to arms, arms to hands, hands to paddle, paddle to water. A circle will be completed. When a circle is complete in the outdoors, medicine can flow. Power can flow, effort given is effort returned. No energy is expended in this closed loop. Motion without effort, a dance with no music, travel without motion. Creating this circle and being contained fully within it connects you to another circle. Once your circle touches the circle of water your medicine will co-mingle.

You will no longer travel, no longer paddle, no longer try. If only for the briefest of seconds that lasts your whole life, you are one of the elements that power this planet. You are water; the most powerful, unstoppable, relentless force on the planet. You are water; passive, graceful, effortless. In fact you are none of these things, because water, at its essence is simple.

It flows, and so will you.

Sweet like harmony made into flesh
You dance by my side, children sublime
You show me continents, I see islands
You count the centuries, I blink my eyes
Hawks and sparrows race in my waters
Stingrays are floating across the sky
Little ones, my sons and my daughters
Your sweat is salty
I am why, I am why, I am why

Bjork- "Oceania"

Four lessons-

Type I Fun-is fun to do and fun to talk about later.

Type II Fun-is not fun to do but fun to talk about later.

Type III Fun-is not fun to do and not fun to talk about later.

Andrew Skurka, "The Ultimate Hiker's Gear Guide"

Lessons from Canoe Country:

On our first trip to the Boundary Waters and Quetico Provincial Park, we had 24 people. If you're not familiar with the place, it's all one big area, the Boundary Waters are on the American side, and Quetico is the Canadian side. There are some minor differences, but a trip to either park or even nearby Voyager will net you the same result. Miles and miles of canoe country.

This is an area that if you drew a one mile line, east west or north south, you will hit at least one lake. Group size is limited to nine, which really means eight. In addition, the area is served by a permit system. I'm not up on the current rules, but generally speaking, you put in for permits on the first of the year if you hope to get in. It's possible, but not likely, to get a permit later in the year, but getting the permits you want is like winning a grand on a scratch off ticket.

We did well in the permit lottery. While some folks balk at such measures, I for one enjoy the system. It keeps the place wild, and it keeps people spread out. We were planning on using an outfitter on Moose Lake, and were fortunate enough to land permits that would allow all three of our groups to leave without taking a shuttle. If you go, get a permit first, and then figure out the rest. I think this adds to the trip, you have to go where they tell you to go. I can't say there is a bad spot to go, but we got some of the best. As I began to put the itinerary and routes together a plan began to take shape.

Two of the group's routes were easy; we landed Sunday Lake and Louisa Lake. Nice, easy to reach lakes just across the border. I know I said it doesn't matter, but I'm a liar. There is something exceptional about paddling across the border. It was personally my first time out of the country. Paddling though customs is also a unique way to leave the country. The Canadian side doesn't have designated campsites, and for some reason feels more remote. Even though it's all the Northwood's, it's somehow different when you're North of the Border.

Five lakes, two portages, and about ten miles got group one to Sunday Lake. Another few portages and a few more miles got group two to Louisa Lake. So far so good. We had a few strapping lads, many out of shape dads, three moms, my girlfriend, and a few younger siblings. About 1/3 of the folks going were in good condition, about 1/3 in the middle, and the other 1/3 were pretty well off the couch or too young to be useful. But we had a week, so even the twenty-eight mile trip wasn't a stretch for the folks in group two. We hadn't designated groups, and wouldn't until we got the final routes together.

For each group, I created detailed routes, with detailed fallback plans. We'd all originally agreed that we didn't want to basecamp and that we wanted to move each day. But you never really know, so for group one I planned a forty five mile trip, with bailouts and options to lengthen or shorten their route as needed. Group two got a fifty mile plan, same deal. Worst case, each group had an option to drop their trip to around twenty miles round trip, slightly stretching the permit rules, but still close enough. Because the lakes were near each other, I included two opportunities to rendezvous, since you can't travel together. I also set things up so we could all meet on the final night, and paddle back to the outfitters together.

Then there was the third permit. Carp Lake. Not a bad permit by any means, but it was due East, the others due North. Whoever took this permit would not meet up with the other groups. But, such is life; I put together a similar trip to the others, and began preparing to divvy up the groups. We had a simple rule, each person could choose a buddy, but not the rest of their group, the buddies would be placed into groups. During the public side of the discussion this was the only fair way to do it, folks were happy.

Behind closed doors, a few people would handle the process, basically my dad, one of the other fathers, and me. There were a few other folks in and out, but the final call was ours. I laid out some options based upon buddies, the rules (girls must travel with at least two female adults, guys with at least two male adults), and we also tried to consider family divisions since we had several families and sets of brothers involved. I had some decent options laid out; I kept the husbands and wives together, dads and sons, sons and buddies. The groups were pretty well balanced; each group had a strapping lad and a healthy dad. Younger siblings, women, and out of shape Dads were spread out. I was pretty proud of what I laid out, presenting three simple options for us to choose from.

I did not do well in the group member lottery. Out of left field, one of the moms caused trouble. Not just for me, but for all 24 people on the trip. The problem was, only the three of us choosing knew it. The bigger problem was I was sixteen. I had a pretty strong voice, but not the final say. My dad got to go with my brother and me, so he was pretty content. I did not get to go with my girlfriend, so I was not. The other dad was a victim, and paid dearly. Instead of three nice groups (and one romantic sub-group), we ended up with one good group and two badly balanced groups. Our group took the third permit, the other two were chosen by coin flip.

Left with this life-ending crisis (I wasn't going with my girlfriend), a new plan took shape, a bold plan. I looked harder at our group. It wasn't perfect, but it was pretty good. My dad was no superhero, but he could paddle a boat and carry a pack. My brother Mike was an athlete, and a good paddler, my brother from another mother, Mike, was strong. Josh Ward was a fit enough lad, his father, a bit of an unknown, but Mr. Ward was a fairly fit fellow as well. Scott and Joe would fill out the group, fifteen, small, but good folks. I put together nearly an eighty mile trip, not some simple jaunt across open water, but a complicated, remote route. There were over forty lakes, several unnamed. There were over thirty five portages, a few of them long.

But it would take us east, as the permit required, then it would take us in a spectacular loop, and finally, it would put us in Louisa Lake on the last night. There we could rendezvous with the other groups; I could sit in Louisa Falls with my girlfriend. It would all work out. It was a HARD route. I knew it was probably out of reach. Unlike the other routes, there were no elaborate backups, no careful bailouts. There was only one. By day three, if we didn't hit our mark, we'd have to turn around. It was a dumb route. It was irresponsible. If different names were on this route I wouldn't let them take it. I wouldn't even show it to them.

But my name was on this route. I was the strongest navigator, the strongest paddler, and the most experienced. And I was sixteen, so clearly we could do it!

Lesson One: Trust yourself.

Group two had some moderate paddlers, but no experts. I know I sound arrogant, but that's your job if you are a group leader or route setter. You have to be cold, objective, honestly assess each member. When you plan a trip you must plan a safe trip. You must plan a trip that meets the needs of the group members, takes into account their abilities, pushes them a little, but keeps the trip in reach. Group two was in good shape, they had a nice route with plenty of options.

So the day before departure we gathered around the map table at the outfitters group by group to review each of their final routes. A staff member from the outfitters joined us to give the route a once over as I reviewed it once more with each group.

The two adult leaders of group two were Wayne Connelly, the vice president of a local college, and Jack Reed. A policeman, who had solved a locally famous murder case which resulted in having a book written about him. Said book was turned into a movie series starring Brian Dennehy. In short, damn fine folks.

Upon finishing the review, the outfitter's staff member pronounced it was sound. Mr. Connelly, a talkative fellow, and Mr. Reed, an observant but otherwise quite silent fellow, looked carefully at the maps. "Well there buddy!", said Mr. Connelly "That does look pretty good, but I think, what we'll do, is just paddle up here, and here, and portage here, and camp on this island here." Should take you a day each way commented the outfitter. "Well Jack, that sounds about right to me, how 'bout you?" "Sounds good"

And just like that, all the careful planning turned into a ten mile each way base camping trip. Not out of sheer laziness, but because they knew themselves, they knew what they were up for, and they trusted themselves. These were two fairly capable fellows, when all the options were laid out, all the "expert" opinions presented, they took a look, gave it some thought. Their option wasn't on there, but they trusted themselves.

Of the three groups, they had the most enjoyable trip.

Lesson two: Never take the wrong group, no matter what.

Group one was a bad group. I knew it. I knew it the second it was proposed, I knew it the whole time. One of the few shouting matches our little leaders group had was over this group. But nothing could be done. The third leader's wife had sabotaged the entire 24 man trip. My dad wasn't going to tell another man his wife was wrong, besides I had already said so. The other man knew his wife was wrong, but had no way out. I was sixteen. So, after review of the route, which was easy enough according to the staff member at the outfitters, Group One headed out. Two sets of husband and wives went. One of these dad's was pretty strong, the other was not. One of the wives was pretty useful, the other was not. Joining this group was another single mother and my girlfriend. Two middle aged men, three middle aged women, and one sixteen year old girl. Since all the moms were in this group, the younger siblings went too, so add two young boys to the group, about thirteen or less if I remember right. No navigator, only one member of the group strong enough to portage a canoe. Not a single person in the group was an experienced paddler.

If I was older, wiser, or smarter, I would have insisted they forget what the permit said, take two days to get up past the border, find a likely spot and base camp. But I didn't, and neither did they. If it wasn't a youth group, we could have been more flexible on the rules regarding female travel. The whole thing spun out of control as a result, my girlfriend had to have two adult women with her. The wife in question refused to go (fine by me) without the other ladies. For her it was a grand adventure with her girlfriends, not the pinnacle of scouting for several young men. But this one person, screwed up the other groups, resulting in six weak members in one group. I think the one dad knew something was up, but he was an easy going guy, his wife and boy were coming along, so no biggie. The other dad was the victim of the railroad job, and had nothing to say.

A third of their group didn't weigh enough to paddle a canoe. The other third wasn't strong enough to paddle a canoe, and the remaining two people did all the work, including portaging four canoes and all the gear each time. Even more astonishing, they kept on the route, ignoring every bailout, turnaround, and option to cut the trip short.

The easy going group member, spent over an hour bitching me out when I landed at the dock of the outfitters. Ironically, it wasn't the first time that week. I took it; I let that group go out. Nobody was man enough to admit to him why his group turned out the way it did. I was sixteen, but I was a grown man. He was a grown up, but honestly, he didn't know any better. When you've been part of ruining another man's vacation, especially when his wife and small boy are along, you accept the yelling. A few folks tried to intervene, but it didn't matter, I planned the trip.

This group had the worst time.

Group three: Our trip was going well. We cleared customs, made it to Carp Lake and by mid-day entered the Man Chain. From that point, until a time roughly six days later, we would not see another soul. That Man, This Man, No Man, Other Man. We headed up to Deadman's Portage near the eastern boundary of the park; we swung around heading north, and began our return loop to Louisa. It was fantastic. We saw it all, travelled swiftly, developed a rhythm on portages, and laughed the whole time. We ate well, had camp after wonderful camp. It was difficult, but I wasn't wrong, we were a good group, we could do it. It was at the edge, but it wasn't our limit. We all knew it too, it was exciting. We saw things we knew the others would not see, reached remote lakes too small to name, but each different, each unique.

We were right on schedule; they were full days, but not a crushing pace. Nobody collapsed on shore; we enjoyed our meals, performed camp tasks, and enjoyed our time together by the fire each night. Most mornings were lazy enough, but still efficient. We moved like a well-oiled machine, each person fell to the tasks that fit them best, and fell asleep each night with the satisfied sleep of the traveler.

On any trip near your limit, something must go wrong. When all goes right things are fine, despite being a little worn out. But when you're worn out, and something goes wrong, it goes really wrong. Mr. Ward was worn out. Jerry was at his limit. On our final night, we reached the north end of Louisa Lake. Right on time, it was midafternoon. Five more miles and we would reach Louisa Falls.

A spectacular fall with a natural bathtub in the middle of a roughly forty foot waterfall. For some visitors to the park, this waterfall is their destination, and because of our permit, because of my girlfriend, I had taken eight people on the most ass backwards roundabout route you could take to reach it. I didn't know it at the time, but the other group never even made it this far, not even by the route that was 1/3 the length of ours. But my plan had worked; we would reach the falls and make our rendezvous.

Except for one thing. Louisa Lake is five miles long, on a nearly perfectly 45 degree bearing, running Southwest to Northeast. It is barely a mile wide, but closer to a half mile wide in most sections. As we reached the northern shore we looked down the lake. We looked into the teeth of a strong wind coming almost perfectly from the southwest. Perfectly whipping five miles of narrow water into whitecaps two to four feet high. There was no way we were paddling down Louisa. I knew it. But I was sixteen, my girlfriend was a two hour paddle away, if I said we could do it, we could do it. So we tried.

I was the best paddler in the group, and it took all my skill to keep the boat pointed forward and moving. The rest of the group were not so lucky. We were six days into a difficult trip, at the end of a long day. I watched as the others struggled, I watched the terror on Mr. Ward's face as his boat nearly flipped as each wave came up. We were barely 100 feet off-shore. My dad called it off, we returned to shore. Jerry was at his limit, Jerry was afraid, Jerry was pissed. I was pissed, we had failed.

On shore, Jerry laid into me. I was too pissed to see it for what it was, but I knew it later. I'd seen the face of a man at his limit. I'd seen the fear, seen the fear turn to rage. I'd put him in that spot.

I was pissed about my plan not working out. I was pissed my group couldn't make the paddle. I was pissed about him being pissed at me. I was pissed at my Dad for calling it off. I was pissed at myself, because this was all my idea. We stopped early that day, we cooked an early dinner. Jerry calmed down. Everyone was happy for the break, for the early day. We had a great meal, went over all the amazing things we had seen. I was still pissed.

It turns out, that the north shore of Louisa Lake is a pretty amazing place. That wind that stopped us dead in our tracks also created something that is exceptionally rare in the Northwoods. Something I have rarely seen since. A true novelty. The north shore of Louisa Lake has a sand beach. Not a little sandy dusting, but a full blown, walk out for a dozen feet sandy beach. Our unplanned stop turned into a beach party. It was unbelievable. When I finally calmed down to see it, I realized why everyone was so happy. The swimming was fantastic, the soft sand warm from the sun. It was beautiful, wonder after wonder greeted us on every turn of this trip, and this beach was no exception. After the difficult trip, a beach vacation was just what everyone wanted. What everyone needed.

Some folks wonder why I love the woods so much. Why I believe they hold some power, some force. Why I think if you spend some time out there, you'll meet it, you'll see it for yourself. For some reason, although we made dinner, started a fire, washed, swam, and changed clothes, we never set up camp. The tents never made it out of the bag, all the gear stayed pretty well packed up, in fact, somebody packed up all the cooking gear, something we never do until the following morning. We were done for the day, we were at camp, but we never set up. It wasn't my call, it wasn't anyone's call. It just never happened. I don't know why.

In late summer in the Northwoods, something magical happens nearly every day. In the morning, the bugs get up, hang out for a bit and move on. In the evening, they come back, presumably from their day's work, attempt to get a meal, and head out after a half hour. The wind wakes up just around breakfast most days. Puts in a steady shift, and as the sun heads for bed, the wind calls it a day too. So, as usual, around sunset, the wind on Louisa Lake headed home. The entire land seems to follow some unwritten schedule, punch some unseen clock. It took a bit, but the water went to sleep too. We hadn't made camp, nobody knew why until right then. Because about an hour after sunset, as we doused our fire and cleaned up, the surface of Lake Louisa turned into glass.

The moon was up, and bright. I don't think you could see more stars from a space shuttle. Quietly, we put our canoes in the water. Even though most of the folks in the group didn't know how, or had never seen the technique, we all began to paddle with a silent stroke. Mars and Venus glowed brightly in the sky. As we got up to speed, we took off. We traveled off the edge of the earth into space.

It would be impossible, but nearly everyone was sure we paddled the five miles in under an hour. Most of us don't remember paddling much past the time we left shore. Everyone remembers the trip as one of the best nights of their life. Everyone was disappointed when we landed back on shore. We spread our sleeping bags and pads out and slept under the stars. We were tired; I think we even had a brief discussion on the subject. In retrospect, I think nobody had the heart to set up our tents. To cut ourselves off from the sky, to officially admit what we'd just experienced was over.

Group three had the most rewarding trip.

Lesson Three: Take the best trip.

Group one had the worst trip, a trip they should never have taken. Group two took the most enjoyable trip, nothing remarkable happened, but they sure had fun. Group three had the most rewarding trip, it took some effort, but it was worth it. So which is the best trip?

I can't tell you.

Only a few people in group one came back the following year, of those that did, they had little choice. The guy who chewed me out? Packed up his family and went to Yosemite.

Group two took a great trip, it was memorable, it was safe, and it was enjoyable. They played it safe, made sure there was no stress. For a first trip, it was a fantastic choice. Everyone in this group wanted to go the following year, and most of them did. None of them basecamped the second time around.

In group three; Mr. Ward was the only one not to come the following year, he couldn't get off work. Not long after getting bitched out by my second adult of the trip, Mr. Ward came up to me and shook my hand, man to man. And then he looked me hard in the face, and gave me a hug, traveler to traveler.

You never want to be in group one. Group two is safe, it's a good trip, and for 75% of the folks out there, I'd say it's the best trip. Even with a little experience, do you want to take a risky trip if you only go out once a year? A risky trip is always a gamble, after this trip I came up with the 80% rule, and use it still today.

As for group three, it may have just been sixteen talking, but I don't think so. I knew, with all my heart, that there was a good chance we could do the trip my group took. The folks that went knew each other pretty well, we trusted each other. We had fathers and sons, brothers, best friends. With the exception of the Wards, the rest of us had been camping together for over five years together, most of us longer. We had the right group, almost the perfect group to take on this risk. I pushed it a bit, got a bit lucky, but the reward was worth the risk.

Perhaps, you could say, the risk was rewarded.

The following year, my group took a safe trip; we paddled out to the Basswood Fall's area, and had a remarkable trip. We'd added more folks to our group; four groups went the second year, thirty two people in all. I planned their trips, I applied my lessons. All the groups took safe trips in balanced groups. The rendezvous' all worked out. There were no complaints. I was yelled at by an adult, but it was a joyful yell as we shot down a small rapid.

We didn't truly basecamp, but it was close. As a group, we didn't have any life shaking experiences. Camped on the Basswood River, we had a fantastic camp that overlooked a small section of class 1 riffles to one side, and the river flowing off to the other. It was a camp you see on the cover of a magazine, a place captured in a painting.

One night, around dusk, I played in my Old Town Pack, dancing on the surface of the riffles. For a short time, for a brief moment, I heard the music of Mason's Ballet, in this case, a Whitewater Concerto. I learned Bill's Truth; his dance is not without music, in the silence, is a song. I danced with that rapid for a time, we spoke of some things; I learned that rewards can come on any trip.

Although we paid each other little attention at the time, my wife was on this trip. The girlfriend of last year's trip had faded away. The reward was not as obvious, the timeline not so quick. My wife swam in the same rapids, the very day after I danced with them. Perhaps they spoke to her as well. Many years later, on the shore of another lake, we would dance this dance together. A few years later, we danced a dance at our wedding. I learned that rewards can come at any time.

Lesson Four:

I love the woods for times like that night on Louisa Lake. When it seems that all of creation has conspired against you, defeated you, beaten you. It's not always so black and white, so quickly resolved. But nearly every time, when you get a chance to look back, you'll often see it was simply somebody doing you a favor, looking out for you. A tap on the shoulder. "Hey, buddy. Wait here a minute, I know you're in a hurry, but there's something you should see." On that day, on that lake, in that place, somehow it all worked out.

Even if it happened only once, I'd still go to the woods. If I felt any differently during the experience, I'd blow it off. I was sixteen, but at that moment, if you'd asked me my girlfriend's name, I wouldn't have been able to tell you. When something like that happens, it can change your life.

It's probably just the simple wonder, the beauty of nature. It's probably nothing special, just a coincidence, one of those random things. Right place right time. Right person right mood. A romantic story, a once in a lifetime experience.

Except it happens all the time.

The Rape-

A float trip on a river is a fine way to spend a lazy day. You don't need much; just a place willing to rent you a canoe, really. A few good friends, beverages of your choice and someplace to keep them at your desired consumption temperature round things off nicely. Swimsuit clad participants are always a welcome bonus. It's the kind of trip that the greatest of long distance hikers and the greenest of aspiring outdoorsman can enjoy alike. On the AT such a trip is so popular that many hikers choose to suspend their hikes for a time and "Aqua blaze" the river adjoining Shenandoah National Park, a welcome vacation from the job their hikes have become.

As a young lad, I was fortunate to be a member of a fine troop of Boy Scouts, even more fortunate to have my father serve as Scoutmaster. Having taken advantage of one of Scouting's wisest practices, we had recently started an Explorer's Post. At age 16 Boy Scouts and Girl Scouts have been determined to have reached an age when they are allowed to form a uni-sex group. Such groups typically have a career oriented theme; law enforcement, fire fighting, aviation, science.

Our group was also founded with a very specific theme in mind; exploration. Specifically of the opposite sex. So the second enough members of our Boy Scout troop had reached the required age we formed a Post and approached girls from school to join up. We would have approached some Girl Scouts but we couldn't find any, despite exhaustive searches for them at every scouting event we had ever attended.

So what better way to get the Explorers Post off to a good start than with a summer float trip on the Fox River in Central Illinois? The river in that area is a popular place, and was crowded as usual. It was a beautiful, seventy some odd degree sunny day with not a cloud in sight. Although (legally) still too young to drink, we could at least take advantage of the typical clothing requirements of summer canoeing and get to know our new recruits better. Most of the crowd were in swimsuits, cliff jumping, drinking, floating, and having a great time, so we blended right in.

Despite the weatherman's best predictions to the contrary, an unexpected summer storm kicked up. Since we were all in rented aluminum boats, we prudently got off the water. As the thunder and lightning started and a light rain fell, temps dropped into the 50's.

Regarding canoes, water, and lightning in combination one might make a halfway logical argument favoring a fiberglass canoe as protection from electrocution, but when talking aluminum even that weak argument fails. While I credit my training as an Eagle Scout with being able to remove myself from a body of water during a lightning storm, most other paddlers that day did not have such training and were fortunate to have my father screaming at them, "When there is thunder and lightning exit the water!" We got a small fire started and continued to call out warnings to the other paddlers as they paddled downstream in an attempt to reach some unknown safe haven.

Within a half hour we had over forty people on shore with us. A few girls in our group were already mildly hypothermic, so we kindled a few bigger fires and got them warmed up and dressed in the warmer clothes we packed along just in case. It's important to be prepared before bringing swimsuit clad women into the outdoors; thankfully the BSA made us wait until we were 16 prior to doing so. As people began to drift in, we began to warm others in need. A second fire was built, a third, and a fourth. We rushed around to assess and treat people as the shoreline turned into an impromptu hospital or party depending on which group you were in. In short order, well over fifty people, half of them hypothermic, at least a dozen dangerously so, were on the shore.

One of my father's long standing and favorite topics of discussion covered during his talks as Scoutmaster was that of hypothermia: A brutally dangerous condition that few people take very seriously. A condition that is often most grave during conditions such as this. When the weather is not something to be taken seriously until suddenly, it is. While the topic had become a long standing joke by all in our troop after years of review and education, like all good running morbid jokes they are seriously funny until suddenly, they aren't.

While the Scouts have fallen out of favor a bit, while they aren't all comprised of fine folks, attentive lads, and good hearts; I knew one troop that was. And while we all prefer to joke about such things, when the time for joking has passed...Well it's really something to see a well-oiled machine spring into action.

I distinctly remember three different guys, suffering moderate to severe hypothermia. Since they were drinking, their symptoms were not overly obvious, as drunken behavior is a sure sign. The most dangerous sign, failure to act, was apparent in each. As they stood shivering violently, under a tree or off to the side, I told them to move to one of the fires and warm up. A dull glassy look and promises to do as told followed. "Sure man, good idea. Why didn't I think of that, I'm freezing." As I came around again, each of them remained in their original position.

When hypothermic, your mind may understand what needs to be done, but you simply fail to act. One of these gentlemen had a jacket on, but failed to zip it up. When it was zipped for him, he would unconsciously unzip it again. Each person had to be physically moved to a warmer position; a healthy person had to be stationed by this person to prevent them from wandering away, which two of them attempted to do frequently.

A very pretty girl was there celebrating her eighteenth birthday. She was with her family, they were all pretty drunk, but enjoying themselves. Everyone on shore was enjoying the girl and her skimpy swimsuit and whispered discussions took place regarding eligibility. She was promptly invited to join the Explorers Post. Unfortunately within a few minutes she was in pretty bad shape. After we warmed up one of the gals in our group, we recruited her to warm the girl up skin to skin and gave her one of our fleece jackets to help her warm up. She recovered well enough to be left alone in about half an hour. But our troubles with her were not over at all.

Since the party was in full swing, and she was celebrating, she somehow ended up smoking up with some scraggly looking dudes in their forties who were out there for the day. Nobody knows what happened exactly, but she was drunk enough and high enough to wander away with one of the guys and fool around a bit. Pretty harmless really, and while I wouldn't have agreed with the fella that she was coherent enough to make an informed choice, she did participate willingly enough by all accounts. Although popular vote among our group after the fact was that they simply snuck away to smoke their joint and at best he stole a kiss on the cheek. Unfortunately her dad and uncle didn't see it that way.

Watching drunk, hypothermic people fight is funny, don't get me wrong. But it was also dangerous considering the precarious state of our field hospital. While it was broken up fairly quickly, partly by the daughter and mostly by my friend Matt, it created a bit of a situation. Irrationality is next on the dangerous conditions checklist; people just do very weird things. Obviously things were aggravated by the booze, but our cozy little encampment suddenly became quite violent, as a small but vocal group led by the now moderately hypothermic uncle began to organize a lynch mob for the rapist.

There was no rape, no one was even sure there was a kiss, and uncle was shivering so violently that he couldn't tie his shoes let alone a noose, but the emotions were very real, and completely rational for these men. A few drunks egged them on, but it was simple irrational behavior brought on by hypothermia that was the real fuel for the fire. Somehow they managed to get a few painters (rope) from the boats and were getting pretty serious. Their seriousness spread among the camp and the world famous telephone game made matters worse as the accusation morphed into rumor, then fact.

So we took the "rapist", and his terrified buddy who apparently just worked with the guy, didn't really know him, and was not prepared to die in his company, and quietly put them in a canoe. We sent him downstream with a few responsible folks to diffuse the mob. The worst of the lightning storm had passed, but a light rain still fell. We cajoled, separated, and spread out the worst of the offenders, and talked dad and uncle into sitting at a separate fire with the forgotten swimsuit model. She had been drinking steadily and was on the verge of blacking out, so we mentioned that they may want to spend a bit of time with their underage daughter and ensure that she didn't die of alcohol poisoning.

Eventually the storm completely subsided, and a few of the rental companies sent some boats up river to help tow people in. Apparently someone had walked to a nearby farmhouse and called the police about the rape, so the rental folks were alerted to our camp. We were on shore for roughly three hours, max. The party broke up, the field hospital was dispersed. By then the temps were back in the sixties. If we weren't there, who knows? But it was a hell of a first trip for our Explorer's Post. We were young boys, so the hypothermia lectures became funny again by the time we were riding home, but the laughter had a little pride in it after that day.

It also locked in for me how quickly all the different factors can set in, and all the scary forms that hypothermia can take on. What a strange thing is that chill breeze that robs you of your mind, your ability, and your will to survive. What a rare thing to see it on such a massive scale, a lynch mob forming over an imagined crime.

A rape of reason.

After reaching the rental place the "rapist" was taken into police custody. The true culprit, hypothermia, fled the scene as usual when the sun came back out. After a few hours, uncle, dad and daughter had sobered up enough to straighten things out. Handshakes were exchanged and no charges filed. The bored cops relegated to river rat babysitters were visibly relieved by the lack of paperwork involved.

Everyone actually turned out to be pretty nice folks, who aren't really sure what happened to them that day.

The Chilly Hiker-

"Too much water," returned Arrowhead, with a slight nod of the head; "Tuscarora too cunning to make fire with water! Pale-face too much book and burn anything; much book, little know."

James Fenimore Cooper. "Pathfinder; or, the inland sea."

The old feller was having a good day. It was decent enough out, mid-sixties, steady rain, but not a blinding downpour like the previous day. He'd made good time, 'bout 20 odd miles so far and though the views weren't great he could see the general condition of things from up on the ridge he was hiking.

There was a front coming in from the north, and it would chase away the rain but cool things off tonight. There was a shelter ahead and dinner time was approaching, it looked like the front would roll in and he could hike a few more hours after dinner and dry out on the move, so as the trail dipped down off the ridge towards shelter and spring the old man began to dream of dinner.

As he reached the shelter he saw gear sprawled out across the shelter, at first the old man assumed that somehow this shelter was equipped with a hidden washing machine that had thrown-up mid load. In the corner he saw it; the wet, lumpy, down bag, the pointy nose attached to the shivering body of some unidentifiable member of the human race that blew his initial theory to pieces.

"Ahoy the shelter" the Ol' Man spoke up. The shivering took on a bit of purpose, a draw cord was loosened on the useless mummy bag, and the nose grew into the face of a young man. "Hello", was all he managed as the old man flopped his pack down on the picnic table. The young man made no other real effort to move, himself or his gear, so the old man thought he should reduce the embarrassment of the young man's failure to make room for a fellow hiker, "Yar, just here for some dinner and then on down the trail, no need to clear a space for me in there young man, the rain should be clearing up shortly."

This perked up the young man a bit, "Thank God, all my shit is soaked." The words came from shivering lips, as the Old man thought to himself, "Mayhap I won't be moving on as quickly as planned."

After filling his water bags the old man began to prepare dinner and inspect the young feller a bit more critically.

"You done for the day fella?"

"Yeah, I had a big day though, 25 miles, and I'm beat, just going to go to bed early tonight"

"No dinner then?"

"No stove for me man, cold food only to keep the weight down"

"Why not start a fire, dry out your stuff and warm up a bit?"

"No time for that, I get up early so I can keep up my miles"

The old man added some more oregano to his soup and shut down the stove, the scent from his meal began to fill the shelter, and the previously mentioned nose of the frigid fellow in the shelter. "Big miles huh? What kinda numbers are we talking there tough guy?"

The young man became a bit indignant at the question, sitting up in his bag to face the old man so that he could shiver away with a bit more dignity. "I'm doing 20's mostly, but I've hit a few 30's when the weather is good or the trail lets me"

"Well, at that pace you should have plenty of time to start a fire at the end of the day, hell you're probably getting to camp by three in the afternoon at that rate!"

The young man's chilly noggin was a bit slow to comprehend the insult, but when it kicked into gear the old man got the response he was looking for, the kid was pissed. "I hike at least 10 hours a day, 12 today actually, and I don't have time for a fire or your shit, so eat your food and move on." The old man stoked the flames a bit more, "Yar, I got 20 something miles so far myself, probably get another six in before bedtime, but I got a late start today, so no big miles for me. Hell, you probably don't know how to start a fire anyway, since you don't have enough sense to dry yourself out and eat a good meal after your *"big day"* I guess it was a bit uncharitable of me to assume you knew what the fuck you're doing."

That one did it, the bonfire the old man was looking for was good and lit, and the kid unzipped his bag and started crawling out. Even the clothes in his bag were wet as he spluttered, "That's enough..."

"Yar, you're up and at 'em now, so sit your frigid ass down on the bench."

The old man could talk with some authority when he wished to; "It's about sixty or so right now. That sopping shit bag of down sponges of yours is about as warm as the fire you didn't start. Even if the wind doesn't change tonight it'll be in the fifties, but problem for you, fella, is that the rain stopped a few minutes back because the wind did change, odds are decent it'll be in the forties tonight, odds are decent you go to bed like that and you won't wake up in the morning. Best case scenario for you is you live through the night, burn all your energy up just to stay alive, and you'll zero here tomorrow to recover. Looks like a coin flip to me, course maybe I could share my tea with you and we can talk it over a bit."

The Ol' Man smiled at the young man, and he smiled inside, too. The kid was afraid now, his bonfire of anger burned down to a bed of coals as the old man's speech played out. The kid sat down, wrapping his hands gratefully around the warm cup of tea as he sipped his first real warmth of the past few days.

A bit more gently he asked him again, "You don't know how, do ya fella?"

"No" the young man quietly informed his cup of tea.

"Well, no shame in that, Ol' Man Willy's my name, and it just so happens I can help you out, maybe it just so happens that's why I stopped for dinner tonight for all I know. Speaking of which, I seem to have accidently cooked two meals here while I was busy flappin' my gums; you better help me eat it up so the critters don't come by looking for the leftovers."

He passed along a helping to the kid, "eat it while it's hot. After dinner I'll show you one of my tip-top personal secrets. I'll teach you how to build an AT fire, it's my own personal invention, free of charge of course, but if we happen to meet at a bar down the road, I'd take it as a great kindness if you could see it in yer heart to buy me a few pints."

The Mountaineer-

"Taking a trip for six months, getting into the rhythm of it, it feels like you could just go on forever doing that. Climbing Everest is the ultimate, and the opposite of that, because you get all these high powered plastic surgeons and CEO's. You know, they pay $80,000 and they have Sherpas who put all the ladders in place and eight thousand feet of fixed ropes. You get to a camp and you don't even have to lay out your sleeping bag, it's already laid out with a little chocolate mint on the top.

And the whole purpose of climbing something like Everest is to affect some sort of spiritual and physical gain. But if you compromise the process: you're an asshole when you start out, and you're an asshole when you get back."
Yvon Chouinard, "180 degrees South" a film by Chris Malloy

On my very first real trip west of the Mississippi I chose to play it safe. I was heading out to visit my dad, and I was fresh off a decent season of hiking. He'd recently moved to the Denver area and a visit for the holidays would let me check out the delights of the fabled outdoor city I had so long heard of. I hopped into my Benz, and fighting a little headwind from the west, made the trip in a sixteen hour shot.

My dad is a bit of an accumulator of things. It's hard for him to pass up a discount bin or fail to justify a purchase. Invention of some halfway plausible scenario where he might someday use an obscure piece of gear is all it takes. I am a bit more direct. When I need something I buy it. Often I will then lend it to some friend or acquaintance, and then be forced to buy something again when I need to use it. My dad is also quite good at inventing reasons to purchase things that I may enjoy or find some use for someday, although occasionally I suspect he simply realizes that he cannot or will not use them and therefore I make an excellent substitute user being his eldest son.

So after I slept off the Benz lag from my long drive it was little surprise to see my father pull out interesting new purchases from odd corners of his slightly cluttered apartment. Now of course such reveals are generally haphazard and slow-going as interesting books or magazine articles are interspersed with wondrous treasures, complete junk, and sundry other goods both brand new or nearing admission to an archaeological museum. Stories of how some particular item was discovered at some remote or obscure roadside store abound. Over the course of a few hours, however, several items quite critical to this tale appeared.

"These, if you can believe it, were just sitting in some guy's garage. Never been worn by all accounts, I found these out on the eastern plains and they were so cheap that it woulda been damn foolish to pass them up." Now I had done a few such trips in my youth, even owned a pair of my own, actually. Though I couldn't tell you which particular friend currently possessed nine-tenths of the law's opinion on their current ownership. I had been ice climbing a few times, and a decent pair of strap-on crampons was once in my quiver of gear. Now what would have been damn foolish is if my pappy strapped these on and went vertical, but that is neither here nor there, for crampons can be quite useful indeed. They'd need a new strap, but unless you really mess something up, well, they're just hunks of metal after all and easy enough to get working again.

"Now this, well, I happened to have a store credit and this was on sale. Figured since I'm living in the shadow of the Rockies it was time to pick up one of these." Now my dad has rarely returned or exchanged an item in his life, so typically "store credit" was code for; "I'm not sure why I bought this exactly but somehow here it is." Now this was a partially practical bit of gear if ever he did seriously plan a hike in more inclement western weather. And it is the sorta thing you could halfway argue, as a former Scoutmaster, mind you, that makes sense to keep in the vehicle if you drive much in the mountains in a "Be Prepared" Scout motto kinda way. But really there was no reason for my pappy to have an ice axe, but there it sat... Bright, shiny, without even the tags or stickers removed. On our few Midwestern ice climbing dalliances I had forgone this particular piece of gear by taking a few bicycle hooks, filing down the tips and screwing them into a few dowel rods. Did the job well enough to get us up a few easy routes.

After a few other items passed through, a few magazine articles were read, and odd books considered, a truly useful piece of kit did emerge. "I love these rich yuppies here, you wouldn't believe what the ski lodge crowd will discard. This was found on a back rack at a shop up in the mountains and somehow it ended up sitting there for only $50!" And indeed this was a treasure.

Back in the days when The North Face was still considered a cutting edge company focused more on alpinism than outfitting city folk for expeditions to the mall, they made some fine gear. This piece was, and occasionally still is, considered one of the finest alpine mountaineering shells around. When a decent used car could still be had for $500 bucks, this jacket retailed for $495 cold, hard, alpine-equipped dollars. The North Face Mountain Jacket was "it," the best you could get, and this one likely had the very history my father imagined. Worn on some corporate ski retreat and discarded once an obligatory run and cocktails with the boss were completed.

So the day fully consumed in the big reveal we headed for books and eventually bed. Now I had brought a few things along in case we wanted to try a quick overnight or even try my hand at a solo trip, but mainly I'd just come to see my dad. No trips were planned. We car toured around, visited a few of his treasure shops, took in the sights and had a fine visit. All the while, though, the items sat near the spot on the floor where I had set up my pad and bag, taunting me with their possibility. On one trip to REI's flagship store, I snagged the strap needed to repair the crampons, and like my pappy often did, came home with something I wasn't sure how I ended up with.

We took a road trip down to Mesa Verde a few days after I arrived, a fine trip for another tale. But eventually we made our way back to Denver and my father had a little work to do. Left to my own devices, I fired up the Benz and took a ride to the ranger station to learn more about Rocky Mountain National Park. After completing a brief driving tour not long after my arrival in Denver, to say the least, my curiosity was piqued.

Now you see, I was once a pretty decent rock climber. It was one of my prime passions and a pretty dominant hobby for a fair bit of my younger days. I went on to teach climbing classes and still get out every great once in a while. Like any climber, the Diamond on Longs is a pretty well-known and world famous wall. Now in the Midwest, there isn't a climb much past 200' tall, so the multi-pitch monsters of the west are a true wonder to me. And while the sport of mountaineering is not of any special draw to me one way or the other, well, these were some mountains.

So I discussed it with the rangers, debated a bit with myself as I stared at it, and finally discussed it with my pappy upon my return. This was supposed to be an easy going trip, a flatlander getting a taste of the Mile High City. But some fool had bunked me down next to crampons, ice axe, and a proper mountaineering shell. And then that idiot had driven me by one of the most famous mountains in the world. Somehow, even after all this, I was left unsupervised for a period of time. It was inevitable, really. Besides, somehow, for no practical reason and without any store credit to spend, I'd bought a map of Long's Peak at REI and it woulda been damn foolish to pass up the chance to use it.

Now I'd been out here a good week and was starting to acclimate to a certain extent. Long's may not be the tallest peak in the Rockies, but it's up there. It may not be the hardest, but I'm not sure on that, to be honest. It's about eight miles each way, with about 5000 feet' of elevation gain. Not the end of the world for an Appalachian Trail hiker, right? And then there's the Diamond, that famous and large looming icon in the world of climbing that haunted me a little bit. Now, not being particularly practical or overly cautious at the time, rather than wisely cut my teeth on some lesser peak or easier route, if I was going to make a go of this mountaineering thing, well I might as well make a go of it.

Ascending Long's is something done fairly regularly by the park's many visitors. In the summertime. And even then it's considered a pretty serious climb, occasionally even a fatal one. In the winter, successful climbs can often be counted on one hand, some winters there are none. Now my father had some inkling of these facts, I had almost no clue. It was a mountain, I was here, I had mountaineering gear decent enough for what I would have considered at the time to be a non-technical ascent. A serious walk, but not exactly requiring a rope and full climbing gear. Just some seriously good clothing, crampons, ice axe and a map. A partner would be handy, but there didn't seem to be one of those lying around.

So after lengthy discussion, a two day, solo ascent was planned. I had brought my winter tent, a VE-25, another fine piece of North Face gear suitable for mountaineering. A good warm sleeping bag, a hefty pack, and an extra pad from my father's collection to supplement the one I had brought. A solid MSR stove and cook kit would solve one issue: no water source, but of course it was winter and there was a whole mountain range filled with snow to melt. A pair of snowshoes was rustled up to get me past tree-line. Several decent hats and gloves were pulled from drawers, nooks, and crannies and that was that.

The safe portion of the trip was ended.

I fired up the Benz, checked in at the ranger station, and headed over to the popular Long's Peak Campground. Typically impossible to score a spot any other time of year, I was the only occupant. At 9400', this camp would easily more than double the highest elevation I had camped thus far. Hell, sleeping on my dad's floor had beaten most of my previous camps. I planned to spend a day there to acclimate a bit more, seeing as this was the highest elevation I had ever reached.

It was pretty nasty, so I wrangled up a picnic table to form a wind block. Which turned out to take two more picnic tables to anchor it down and prevent the wind block from crushing me in the night. You know, because it was windy. I pulled a few of those books I mentioned and settled into my tent for a good solid session of acclimation. I felt like a regular Himalayan adventurer working my way from camp to camp up the mountain.

If all went well I would rise early and make my way to tree-line, then head up via the Keyhole Route. I planned to make camp at the shelter there, or perhaps just downhill in the Boulder Field. This way I wouldn't have to start too early, and would have the best chance of making a relatively rested trip to the summit from my planned high camp. I'd be able to stash most of my gear in the tent there for the summit bid the following morning, or even spend an extra night if conditions were bad for a summit attempt.

I sure planned like a regular Himalayan adventurer on some desperate summit bid. I suppose for me and my level of experience it was for the best. Despite a rather cavalier attitude about this sort of thing, I did try to stay fairly rational and practical about danger, provided you ignored the irrationality and foolishness of the pretense for me being in such a situation in the first place. It's good to have some balls from time to time, but once you've pulled 'em out and left 'em flapping in the breeze; best to come up with a solid plan and safe as possible course of action to ensure they're intact for the next adventure.

So after my acclimation day I rose just before dawn. I got a good warm meal stowed away, secured the Benz and headed out. After a pretty straight forward snowshoe up the trail I reached a small wooden bridge and the end of civilization. A sign informed me that this was it, the end of the ranger's responsibility or concern for you or your safety. This time of year, nobody else would be coming past the sign, and it was highly suggested you do the same. Thanks for stopping by, cross this line and we'll pick your body up come spring thaw if there's anything left.

Not far after that the tree-line began to assert itself a bit more rigidly and it was time to remove my snowshoes and stash them on the side of the trail. I'd need to be a bit careful to find this little bit of trail on the return trip, so I secured the bright red shoes to the uphill side of one of the last of the trees to help me find the way out. In theory, I should be able to follow my own tracks out, but as I saw no other tracks on the windblown land it didn't seem like something to stake your balls on when returning wearily from the summit.

It was a decent call, the snow on this windblown land was quite thin, in many spots non-existent. Being on the lee side of Mt. Lady Washington the wind was unpleasantly acceptable and I pressed on. I appreciated the irony of skirting Mount Washington's wife after having climbed her husband in the Whites. It took some effort to get up to Granite Pass, where the trail turns south, but the breathtaking scenery was a welcome companion that made the journey easier. Like many western climbs, this one formed a roughly golden ratio spiral around the peak to spread the elevation gain out.

As I rounded the bend and made my way into the Boulder Field proper, the mountaineering trip began in earnest. The first steep section of this triangular section was not too bad, but the wind was not in my favor. Racing across the range and funneled through The Keyway and hemmed in by the appropriately named Storm Peak and Mrs. Washington it easily raced along at speeds my Benz was likely incapable of. As I came over the initial rise to the relatively flat portion my progress was halted in near comical fashion as I leaned drunkenly forward at an angle that would spell sure trouble for one's nose if not propped up by a wind almost as solid as the mountain above me.

There were occasional large rocks to shelter behind as my pace dropped into yards per hour territory. I found myself ducking behind them every 10-15 minutes and reviewing the map. It was quite silly really, The Keyhole up slope was clearly visible and no map was needed. On one such stop the mountain was kind enough to remind me of this. Whoomp. A gust ripped over the rock and I found myself staring in disbelief at the two scraps of map that remained in my tight grasp. The rest had simply disintegrated into thin air.

After a few more boulder hops the wind once more pulled an impossible feat. I was wearing one of those sweet $60 a pop North Face Windstopper hats with the ear flaps and sturdy drawcord. This was over two more hats and expertly secured under my bomber shell equipped with a three axis adjustable articulated hood designed for an instance just such as this. Unimpressed by mankind's technological wonders, with a whoomp, my hood was ripped from my head and a $60 kite was seen for a brief bit against the dull grey sky as it began a journey back to the fine town of Boulder.

Such setbacks are bound to plague any successful mountaineer, so I dug a spare shirt from my pack and improvised another hat while huddled in the shelter of another rock. I got myself together and once more proceeded. If I could reach my goal I could perhaps get a camp together and make a push on the morrow when hopefully conditions would improve.

Despite the struggle, my current surroundings were quite unique in my experience. Winter is a still time in any area. Being above tree-line an often lifeless desert to my Midwestern eyes. This windswept and nearly snow-free landscape was something else entirely. The bleak, flat, toneless sky a leaden monotonous grey. The rock-scape an almost toneless wash of texture with no pigment. A black and white photo I moved through on a planet normally so vividly colored that it threatens to damage your retinas.

Nothing stirred but the wind, it's relentless motion not so much of a howl as a noiseless blanket swallowing the sense of hearing and rendering me deaf. No life existed but my own. Nothing. Sheltered by the surrounding peaks I could not see out of this small valley. I was alone in a way I had never experienced. Sight rendered nearly useless in this unvaried landscape. Sound lost to the wind. Smell and taste rendered pointless in the snot freezing temps. Touch buried under layers of technical apparel critical to maintaining life.

The stumbling clumsiness as my clunky, stiff, insulated boots attempted to traverse the meteor blasted moonscape. Muscles atrophied by the strange falling, floating, near weightless condition of swimming through the densely steady wind. My ears struggling desperately to find any sound, causing my breathing to take on an oxygen tank feel as deep breaths moved internally and echoed off my skull.

Somewhere between the last sheltering boulder and my next step I had managed to leave the planet and set foot on the moon.

Whoomp. "Hngh." I was on my back, which seemed strange as I was, a moment ago, on my first moonwalk. Some strange disruption in the delicate forces and strange gravity of this new planet had resulted in this ninety degree change in perspective. I lay for some time as my mind analyzed this new information and entered it into the awayship Captain's Log. Hopefully Spock could run an analysis and make future course corrections. Prior to firing boosters and returning to zero degrees on the Z-axis I looked to my right in admiration, "Man... Uhura's legs are fantastic."

I sighted The Keyhole once more, hoping to reach Lunar Station Agnes Vaille and take a critical break to refuel my one man rover. I was unfamiliar with measuring distance in parsecs. In earth units I believe I was still moving at a steady yards per hour pace as I drifted from boulder to boulder, using their relative gravity to anchor my progress. Pushing off from one I would float untethered through the space in between. As my propulsion slowed, it seemed as if I reached some delicate balance just prior to entering the gravity of the next boulder as it sucked me into its orbit in relief.

Whoomp. Again. I examined my space suit for damage, my oxygen tank of a pack once more protecting me from the worst my elbow had stingingly caught the edge of a rock during this shift in gravity. I pressed on before dwelling on the issue overlong and made a few more boulder hops as I neared The Keyhole. But the nearby orbiting peaks had warped the universes gravity field. It was like standing on the backside of a black hole as the entire contents of western space was sucked in and ejected. I made a few bold steps to The Keyhole and the last frontiers of space.

Whoomp! Being a bit more prepared at this point, I had time to realize that I hadn't simply collided with the ground, but had actually been flung off the surface for a brief bit prior to violent re-entry. Bones jumped on the communicator this time, "Dammit Jim, look around you!" This area of space was a vast asteroid field of destruction. One wrong propulsion thrust and I would crash into one with disastrous results. The next collision could easily damage the central computer adding another puddle of lifeless grey matter to the surrounding rocks. Or I could rupture a fluid vessel and lose all propulsion. Much like the departed explorer, Agnes, the lunar station was named for, the vast, sucking cold void of space would drain the life from me as well. More likely though, a broken hip strut would cripple the ship, spelling death for me as surely as the man who died trying to rescue Ms. Vaille. Such an asteroid floated inches from each hip.

They say, "Third time's a charm."

General wisdom regarding this route, regardless of season, is to make a call at The Keyhole. Evaluate conditions, timing, assess your ability, and make the choice to continue or not. The sign near the bridge is simply a formality, a lawyer's warning to be quickly ignored. The Keyhole is the true point of no return. Mountaineering, much like running a dangerous river, has such checkpoints. Few other pursuits do. You don't need to heed them, but your odds of telling the story at a bar are vastly diminished should you proceed. It's this lure, this temptation to proceed, that causes many to perish in pursuit of a tale fit to earn you a lifetime of free drinks.

A much lesser known saying amongst some adventurers:
"Fourth time- you're dead."
Abort mission.

Thump! The instant I called it and stood up facing downhill I found myself back on Earth. It was incredibly disorienting. With the wind at my back walking became easy, even desperately insistent as the mountain reached out with its massive hand and patted me on the back, nearly tumbling me down to Granite Pass. I stopped for a brief break as I rounded the bend and took in the breath reviving views of the Earth spread out before me.

I performed one last task reserved for the mountaineer, my first true, and quite pleasant glissade. I shot down the little snow covered pocket of snow that banked up on the lee side of Mills Moraine. I steered towards the snow shoes I had left near the tree-line and with all senses restored to prime working condition I flew down the mountain. Nearly ten hours of slow struggle to glimpse The Keyhole and I was back down in what felt like an hour.

One of my father's great finds, and long standing companions through my early life, was the Benz. Leather, sunroof, stereo, the works. A finely tuned luxury machine. The Benz had been dropped at one of his customer's auto shops, the massive repair bill left half paid. So in his artful way he negotiated a little horse trading and a payment of $2,000 to settle the bill. And so it came to be that I owned a luxury auto with all the fixins'.

Granted, much like the $20 canoe he had picked up, it had a few holes in the floor. Much like the canoe it was twenty years old. But the repair bill had been to completely rebuild the engine, so despite age and being a few good stomps away from having the Flintstone's propulsion option, it was a good car. A bit of fiberglass and long weekend of squirming on our backs fixed up both the canoe and Benz with equal effectiveness. I share this with you mainly because I now faced a problem few Himalayan explorers face when ending their struggles with the mountain; parking a car at 9200' for several days in sub-zero temps generally will render said vehicle's battery inoperable.

While I had returned very much alive my Sherpa had expired while awaiting me at Camp 1. No phone and the still deserted campground meant that a long wait or walk out was a good possibility. I removed the fuel filter and warmed it with body heat, the Benz being expertly engineered for such field resuscitation efforts. You see this Benz was none other than the legendary 200D, the D standing for diesel which has an unfortunate tendency to gel into a paste in such temperatures.

In addition this fine vehicle was a manual, the mountain would kindly serve as the defibrillator paddles to push start this noble beast. So with some serious effort, and a gentle pry with the ice axe to pop the tires into motion I got the Benz rolling as I hopped in and muscled the atrophied manual steering to point that famous hood ornament downhill. As the Benz got up to speed I dropped the clutch and my companion shuddered to life!

The Benz and I headed back to spend a final night with my much relieved father who was nervously awaiting news. Returning borrowed gear that would be useless back home and loading up new treasures I concluded my visit. I parted ways with my oldest friend, one time Scoutmaster and wily shopper the following morning. With the mighty wind at our backs the Benz flew home in a mere fourteen hours, leaving time to stop by the pub and visit with Ol' Man Willy.

I recounted my adventures to him over a few pints. Good enough for him to listen politely, but not good enough for him to pay the tab, he was nonetheless a good companion to review the lessons and pleasures of the trip. Once it was all spilled out, he gave me a pat on the back as he looked up from his pint and shared some advice.

"There is a saying amongst mountaineers, you know. A fine bit of wisdom it seems you've had a taste of when you faced the 'Point of No Return', and made the right choice." He took a long draught of black draught and passed the saying along, "They say, 'Any asshole can climb a mountain, but it takes a mountaineer to return to camp safely.'"

I digested the wisdom of this statement, one I had heard as well but never truly understood until this moment as the Ol' Man had summed up the moral of my tale. Gladdened by the value of this lesson sincerely learned, I raised my pint in a toast, "To Mountaineers!"

His pint remained on the bar, his eyes distant, perhaps contemplating some old adventure. As my toast went un-cheered I lowered my arm back to the bar.

After a moment he returned and looked at me with a smile, "You haven't climbed shit." He stood, hefted his pint, put an arm on my shoulder and raised a more accurate toast.

"To Assholes"

Wrong Way-

"Any man may blunder once, when confronted by strange conditions; but none will repeat the error unless he be possessed by the notion that he has nothing new to learn."

Horace Kephart, "Camping and Woodcraft"

It was my last day in the Smokies and I had a lot to think about as I got up early that morning and prepared to have a big day, the kind of big day I would need if I was to honestly pursue a speed hiking record. So as I skipped breakfast and packed I donned my rain cape like a superhero and prepared to meet the day.

The misty morning hiking went well, and while it wasn't 5:00 AM, I'd at least gotten off to a more respectable start time than in recent days. I tried hard to soak up the last of the ridge walk views. As I began a descent off what I thought would be the last peak before the plunge. I tried to think back to the missing sheet from my guide book set I had torn off.

I had somehow lost the page for this section of the trail, but the guys from the night before had let me review their sheet; a few miles of ridge walking and then a steep plunge into the gap where I-40 crossed the trail.

I must be there, I figured, as I took in my "last view" of the Smokies; a misty morning where the mountains gave off their namesake in wispy trails that fed the mornings clouds.

I looked down at the survey marker as I shouldered my pack and its inscription caught in the corner of my eye. "5849" was the elevation. Five, eight, four- nine. Shit. I walked downhill another fifteen minutes until I couldn't ignore it any longer. I knew that number. I pulled out my compass, south-ish was the reading, but that often means little on a twisting trail like the AT. But that number, that meant something.

I had no map, once more regretting that ultra-light concession to travel. I was missing the page I needed. The one that would have told me upon later review that I had failed to pass Cosby Knob Shelter. But I did have my memory, and my Jobs-a-ma-phone, which is purported to be quite smart.

With horror I began to flip through my camera roll. I had only taken one picture of an elevation marker over the last 250 plus miles, something I rarely do at all. But the trail had compelled me to take this picture, and it would reveal the sad news.

A wrong way. My first. Ever. While some unfortunate hikers earn trail names like Wrong-Way, U-turn, and Lost-One, that has never been my luck. No one has an inborn sense of direction, but my time in Scouts and as our troop's navigator in the Boundary Waters had ingrained the skill of finding one's way deeply in my being.

It's not that I have never been misplaced, that happens to us all. But a long ingrained habit of checking for a passing landmark not long after any junction had always prevented this sort of thing from lasting more than a few minutes- but no map, no data sheet, no double-check.

So I used the trick that has never failed; I reviewed the day.

I had gotten up early, packed up and left the shelter, recalling the brief conversation I had with "the ladies" my shelter mates: "Well you're out early!" one of them commented. As I donned my superhero cape, I put on my best superhero voice and replied, "Actually Ma'am, I'm running late."

What a douchebag.

I had left the ladies, walked to the trail and took a left. Wrong way.

I climbed back up to the marker and took out my phone. I bent over the marker to compare it to the photo. After all, it was possible there was another 5849' on this ridgeline.

Renowned tracker and wilderness school instructor, Tom Brown, Jr., leaned over my shoulder "Note the slight deterioration of the dead leaves in the photo and their relative positions. But there by the word survey is the giveaway, those two triangular marks could only have been made as a male hiker, 5'8" and one hundred and sixty pounds, with a thirty-eight pound pack stepped off the trail to let two ladies pass. These marks were made by a piece of hard rock caught in the lugs of his size 10.5 Asolo hiking boots. One mark as each lady passed. There is no doubt, this is the same marker."

"Jumping June bugs, Batman!" Robin replied over my other shoulder, "We don't need the Riddler to puzzle this one out! We're on the wrong track!" Another matching photo of the views from the ridge confirmed the truth and pushed the doubt-o-meter back to zero.

After a few minutes of hiking I laughed at myself and replied to the boy wonder, "Well old chum, sometimes you are Christian Bale, and some days you are Adam West."

"To the Batcave."

Getting to the Trail-

"The world is a book, of which those who do not travel read only a page." - St. Augustine

You busy watching me, watching me
That you're blind baby, you neglect to see
The drugs coming into my community
Weapons coming into my community
Dirty cops in my community
And you keep saying that I'm free...
Jill Scott, "Watching Me"

At 2:45 AM local time I sat down on the curb at the Pilot Gas Station at Carbondale Road in Dalton, Georgia and cracked a room temperature Coors Light. Lucky thirteen on the day since leaving my house at 8:00 AM the previous morning and I raised a toast to the bus driver as he drove away. Every good trip should begin with a beer, and every long ride on public transportation should involve another dozen of its closest friends.

About thirty minutes earlier my Greyhound, scheduled to arrive in Atlanta at 3:00, made an unscheduled stop. Most likely due to a premature emptilation of the driver's coffee cup. I took out my Jobs-a-ma-phone five and asked the Japanese girl who lived inside how far it was to Amicalola Falls State Park.

"There are several places to purchase Coca-Cola in your area, would you like directions to the closest one?" "Stupid Bitch." I replied. "Now, now" my not so smart phone chastised me. If only they had spent more time working on teaching the Japanese girl more English instead of witty responses she might be useful.

Forced to go old school (2012 era), I typed in the location on the map and hoped for a signal. Sixty some miles was the result, which seemed a hair better than the eighty miles from Atlanta, not to mention the daunting prospect of walking through downtown Atlanta at 3:00 AM when I would eventually arrive. To cut costs on the trip I cut out the cost of a shuttle to the park, since it was a tune up trip I could use the exercise anyway. As country roads are always more fun than getting arrested walking down the side of the highway, the bus also experienced a premature emptilation of one of its passengers at Dalton.

After lucky thirteen was down for the count I filled up my water and lumbered down the deserted country roads with about eight and a half days worth of food, a pretty impressive feat for a roughly 25 liter homemade pack in my opinion. I had an hour or two's worth of cat-napping on the bus so I worked my way over to the town of Nicklesville by around seven o' the clock.

A short visit from the local law dawg to check me out and register my driver's license in the state's official wandering vagabond database along the way was the only eventful encounter. (I look trustworthy, I don't know why he stopped me?) I was told there was a breakfast place there with homemade biscuits, which turned out to be a gas station, but did indeed have a fella in the back making fresh biscuits so I sat down for a proper traveler's breakfast on the bench outside.

Hydration is always key, as is a gentle transition from an alcohol based system to a water based system. So I bought another beer, a chocolate milk, and a coffee to go with my biscuits. The young lady behind the counter didn't think twice about my order, but in stunned disbelief asked, "Is that yer phone mister?"

You see I carry my phone in a hot pink case. As a practical matter, hot pink is the easiest color to spot should I drop my phone in the woods, and besides, as I explained to the gal before me, "Nobody steals a hot pink phone." Forget the beer and chocolate milk 7:00 AM breakfast order, based on her reaction it appears the most scandalous thing a fella can do in this neck of the woods is carry a pink phone.

I took a little time to repack myself and with a little over a quarter of the distance to Amicalola down I headed over to the bustling center of town (two gas stations and a mechanic's shop) and thought I'd try my hand and pretty legs at flagging down a ride.

And thus began the improbable series of hitches you can only get in the rural south. A mechanic raised in Ohio picked me up first, and explained the differences between the Midwestern fellas and the southern folk (which I will keep to myself). But all in all he was a happy fella down there and took me over near the Carter's Lake area where he had to turn south. After a bit of time there I gave up and road walked a few more miles to slightly more favorable locale by the lake entrance itself hoping to catch a fellow camper instead of the loggers and chemical haulers that kept rolling by.

I snagged a backpacker who worked as a carpenter in the area (that's what I do, more or less) and we talked shop, local codes and hikes. He took me up to East Ellijay where he thought I'd have better luck, and since that's where he was going, well I guess I was too. After getting chased off an abandoned looking lot by a fellow that came out of a very abandoned looking place my first attempt at urinary relief was thwarted. A short road walk solved that problem and I put another mile in to a pull off where I could waggle my tree trunks at the ladies and hope for a ride.

Hook, line, and sinker, I snagged a true rural belle and the real fun began. She had a car that made a beater look nice, a radio with no antenna but she wasn't going to let that stop her from finding a station. Twenty-five years old; three kids, two fathers, neither of them around. Rough morning because Mom is in the hospital with the lung cancer, she explained as she lit her third cigarette in fifteen minutes.

She was running late for work because she was on court ordered random drug tests three times a week for prescription pills and they called her in this morning. She was clean as a whistle now she assured me as we took a slight detour up to a vacation cottage she managed to pick up cleaning supplies so she could get another property ready. She took the mountain roads at 65 and assured me she knew 'em real good as she saw me grab the door handle in alarm. As we raced up a tight winding road in the middle of nowhere she assured me that she wasn't taking me up to do me in or some crazy hillbilly shit like that. "As long as you don't have a wood chipper up there I think we're okay." I noted aloud.

"What'd be the fun in that," she laughed, "then we couldn't torture you or nothin'." "You gotta go toes first, that way I'll make plenty of noise and you can use the hand brake to make it take a while if you like. You're not too well versed in hillbilly tourist killing are ya darlin'? That's the way to go, you get your torturing, choppin', and disposal all done without so much as a mess on your cowgirl boots. Run yourself a little green wood though after me and she'll be all cleaned out and ready for the next fella." I was fairly sure 99% of the conversation was a joke as I waited in the car while she ran into a nice looking summer home to get the supplies.

The obligatory stray dog that seems to be a constant presence in the south came over and checked me out as I waited in the car. On the way back down she finally got around to asking what I was doing, and I told her. The concept of backpacking was not on her radar, so she asked where I was from instead. I live in the south suburbs but I just go with Chicago instead to avoid all the complications. Upon hearing the news she almost killed us for real.

"No Shiiiiiit! I cannot F'ing (she censored herself) believe I am meeting somebody from Chicago today! That makes my day mister and I just cannot believe it. You're really from Chicago then? For real?" "Real as the rock you stubbed your toe on." A nice one I picked up from a hiker from the south on a previous trip. Using the local lingo was as good as showing her two forms of ID and a utility bill.

As we made it back to the highway she explained that with her mom and all she had taken a few pills the other day, but she took a flush and figured she'd be fine but she wanted my "professional" opinion as a big city fella. I've not a drop of experience with any of that mess thankfully and said I had no idea. "Don't matter, the flush always works." And at that point I couldn't decide if they should take her kids or not.

She drove me out to the entrance of the park, a full half hour out of her way, but she said talking to me and doing something good made her feel good. We had some more discussions on various topics I don't need to share, and I hope none of you think I'm putting this girl down. She was a sweetheart that grew up in the wrong place at the wrong time. If any of you reading this have travelled much you know how few options, and how bad things are in any poor rural area.

Good people in a bad place. No matter the color or geographical relation to the Mason-Dixon things are pretty bad. The poorest hiker on their worst day has it better than most of these folks, especially the younger ones. Next time you catch a shuttle or hang out in a town and you get a chance you'll get to talking to the older folks. You'll get to hearing how meth and pills are wiping out all their kids and the grandkids that inevitably show up.

She refused any money, because that "wouldn't be right." I told her I knew she was having an awful bad day, but she made my day a perfect one. "Well that's just something at least. Me making a fella from Chicago's day."

"What is this place anyway?" she asked me. "This park has the highest waterfall east of the Mississippi in it, and at the top there's a trail that you could walk clear on through to Maine; passing D.C., New York, Boston and any town along the way you could think of." Something broke in her a little, "I never even knew..." she said in wonder. "Pack up the kids and bring up a basket for lunch next time you get a chance, maybe bring your Momma. A waterfall is a good place to wash away your troubles." I could tell she didn't really want me to go, but go I did.

The rest of the day was fairly uneventful, the climb was challenging, but the falls, new area and start of trip high we all get made the walking pleasant enough, if not downright wonderful. As I approached Springer I got a little bit of the butterflies I'm sure we all get when approaching this monumental landmark in the world of backpacking. If the Appalachian Trail is not the best backpacking trail in the world, it is easily the most famous. That said, I nearly walked right by it!

Springer is an unassuming summit; tree covered with its small boulder, (by AT standards), at the summit. If a day hiking couple had not been sitting at the rock reading the journal I may well have cruised right past. While this was my first time there, since it was only a tune-up trip I didn't have the same monumental and humbling experience that a starting Northbounder must experience. I signed the journal with my simple name for this trip, "Just Bill". I was nobody special, not a thru-hiker.

I chatted with the couple a bit and got to experience the wonder and awe of an outsider as they read the entries filled with hopes, dreams, anxieties and joys of those beginning their hikes. I also began to understand the fascination that outsiders have in reading hiker's online trail journals, curious how the trips went and what happens to these unknown adventurers who begin the trek. "How far do they make it? How are they doing? Where are they going? What have they seen? And most important of all, who will they become?"

I assumed the pose and put my foot by the handsome patina of the plaque and the first blaze of the trail. While it is a humble mountain I was nonetheless greeted by a pleasant view from the summit, and I considered that perhaps the stunning contrast between Springer and Katahdin is appropriate indeed. Standing here a Northbounder must realize that they deserve no grand send-off to their trip. The mind expanding vistas at the northern terminus and the simple wooden sign that often brings a finishing hiker to their knees faster than a Catholic at high mass wouldn't be appropriate here. The limited view here offers a glimpse of what is possible, but not yet achieved.

I continued down to Springer Mountain shelter; it was late afternoon and I planned on having some dinner and pushing on. The trail however has its own private schedule. Kind enough to wait patiently while I finished my meal and chores the sky steadily darkened giving me a stern but timely warning that it was time to head to the shelter. I had expectations of a quick and passing summer storm, but as I was to learn over the next week, such typical mountain behavior would not be forthcoming in these temperamental times of our earth's moods. I awoke at 5:30 PM after a stealthy nap-monster attacked me, my immune system compromised by nearly thirty six hours of wakefulness, too many beers, and the heavy rains on the roof of the darkened shelter.

All in all, since walking out my front door the previous morning I had traveled from the hum-drum south suburbs of Chicago to the start of the greatest trail in the world in a mere thirty two hours. I find it unsurprising that rocket engineer Ray Jardine chose to pursue his own space program in the woods rather than in town. One of the greatest wonders of any walk is that in such a short period of time we can transport ourselves off the face of our own little world and onto the surface of another planet.

I ended my day with some hope for those folks I had met in the South, as a young boy and middle aged woman joined me at the shelter for the evening.

One of those young grandmothers, was out with one of those unexpected blessings I spoke of earlier. While things are often grim in town, hope springs eternal as always on the trail as this slightly beleaguered but dedicated woman introduced another young soul to the wonders and opportunities afforded to those who travel.

No Water in Shenandoah-

On the first part of the journey,
I was looking at all the life.
There were plants and birds and rocks and things,
There was sand and hills and rings.
The first thing I met, was a fly with a buzz,
And the sky, with no clouds.
The heat was hot, and the ground was dry,
But the air was full of sound.

America, "Horse with no name"

The Ol' Man and Coyote Thunder Owl were moving southbound together through the tropical heat of the Shenandoah. The dense canopy there traps the humidity, so even at a relatively mild eighty-some-odd degrees it was quite saucy. Mainly barbeque, but a fair bit of sweet and sour was in the mix.

But the Ol' Man had had a good bath, a shower and even did some laundry at the lodge the evening prior. He'd also gone down to the restaurant where a fine meal was had during which a few folks had noted his pack. One thing led to the next and a few tales were shared along with a bit of advice on the hiking itself. Said advice led to a few rounds drank in company and paid for by said company. So long story long, the Ol' Man was in a fine mood (even if a bit hung over) this morning when they left the lodge and began another steamy day in the jungle.

A rattler was hogging the trail and seemed unmoved by the plight of these two travelers who only wanted to pass by. A steep drop to the right and a serious slope to the left, meant little room to negotiate this temporary impasse. After a tense standoff wherein the subjects of this story calmly explained that no harm would come to the rattler by allowing the travelers to pass unmolested; a rough truce was negotiated. The rattler recoiled itself roughly a foot off the center of the trail and said adventurers proceeded approximately one foot off the trail on the uphill side.

Coyote Thunder Owl thanked the snake for its kindness and the Ol' Man was in too good a mood to curse the belly crawler's obstinate delay. It was a fine day. The two old friends fell into easy conversation as the miles eased by. Nothing of stupendous note passed them, but there was a wholesome peace within this thin ribbon of woods on this fine sunny day. The Ol' Man had been hiking a bit more frequently with Coyote Thunder Owl, and he began to understand a hair better the connection that led to flashing through the woods so fast that it was slow.

He'd been working on it, because, let's be honest; lazy old men such as he don't really want to expend an exorbitant amount of energy doing anything. Let alone walking through the woods. So, in part, because he found the easy peace pleasurable (what old fellow doesn't enjoy his peace) and partly because it got him to the next beer faster; the Ol' Man was studying on the smooth mode of travel the younger man tended to use. It was tough to do with any regularity (as are a great many things at his age), but when he could slip into the woods and ease across the miles... Well, why not?

So the two fell into an easy pace, conversing indirectly on the very subject of time travel as they strolled along. The Ol' Man wanted to know how to beat the ever sucking, dripping, draining humidity. Coyote Thunder Owl seemed to have a handle on it and was little bothered (he was little bothered by anything really) but the Ol' Man could count no less than five separate rivulets of sweat coalescing into a vast torrent meeting somewhere around his taint before pooling and choosing a leg to follow into his shoes. While they discussed the subject that sneaky, confounding, young man used their conversation to distract the Ol' Man from his discomfort. Instead they discussed the pleasant parts of their day and how the dense air seemed to hold everything still.

See how the spider's web hangs soft and still? The standing ones drink in the heat? The winged ones sit softly singing their conversations? Even the beams of sunshine seem to pause and laze in the air? All are slowed by the air so dense it is as if they swim through it. So too must we flow. Be as the water, dense in form but freed from the ground as the summer's heat allows you to take to the air and flow over the land. Concentrating your strength as the arms of the standing ones stop you from drifting to the heavens, forcing you to flow along the contours of the earth. Rather than fight the conditions, seek instead to emulate them.

Well, truth be told, the Ol' Man had only the slightest inkling of Coyote Thunder Owl's mystic mumbo-jumbo. It was humid, and everything seemed to hang its head low under its oppressive weight, even the humidity itself. But the young man did have a soothing voice. Enveloped in it, even an old man must concede, there was something peaceful about the whole deal if you let it be. So the ol' fella let the weight of it settle on him. Like a wave of steam washing over in the sauna he let the invisible, but quite tangible, blanket settle on him as he drifted away. As the heat settled into his old bones they seemed to limber up and unlock. The miles fell away as he was absorbed into the air hanging along the trail.

Some infinite time later they came up to a junction. Rather, they arrived at a junction that shook the pair from their flash of travel. The Ol' Man pleasantly noted that, with some effort, he could recall passing several junctions and effortlessly choosing the correct ones. However he also noted that he had drank some three liters of water as he drifted along and the reason to take note of this junction was that it was nowhere near a chance at a refill. In fact with a slight bit of effort he recollected running dry some many hours (or minutes, or days) past and was indeed dangerously thirsty. He was a bit foggy at the moment but the map and guidebook clearly confirmed that it was several miles and hours to the next water source from where the pair stood.

"What's the meaning of this?" the ol' fella demanded of his companion, "you plumb walked me dry. I thought you were in charge of what was what." Crap. The Ol' Man had messed it up again, it seemed. While an otherwise pleasant companion most of the time, Coyote Thunder Owl had a rather unpleasant habit of smiling knowingly and leaving the poor old fella to fend for himself from time to time. This appeared to be one of those times. "Just because you have glimpsed how to travel without a care in the world, does not mean you don't have a care in the world." And with that cryptic bit of advice (if you'd call it that) the young man moved away leaving the old man to fend for himself.

"I suppose that I got any advice at all is an improvement." said the fella under his breath, followed quickly by the accumulated wisdom of this pragmatic and practical outdoorsman, "No way out but out." Somewhat reluctantly, and a bit dizzily we might add, the Ol' Man began to climb the four mile or more up and over that led to the next possible water source. Possible in that at this time of year it may be quite dry, which would be insulting at the least, fatal at worst. Likely his true predicament lay somewhere in betwixt these two extremes; but when you've had an evening of entertaining, a day of dripping buckets, and no likely relief in sight: one can never be too confident in the outcome.

Speaking of confidence, it reached an all-time low when the low spot promising water turned out to be a late season liar.

While pragmatic as always, the ol' fella was practical as well. With another few miles of trail to the next source and his pace hovering in the one to two mile per hour range at this point things were, succinctly speaking, not good. After cursing his traveling chum for a time he realized how simple this stretch would have been if only he had noted the proper intersection and refilled prior to noting the failure to accomplish such a simple task. He supposed, "I suppose all the practical bits and pieces of habit that have kept me in gainful habitation on this planet thus far should not be chucked aside with the first easy-travelling youth I encounter."

So, resigned to the predicament he found himself in, he pulled out his newfangled waterproof map of the surrounding area. He resolved to locate his best shot at a drink and proceed with what meager supply of energy remained. The map's finely colored surface, however, revealed little in the way of relief. The brown lines denoting topography indicated little hope in not only the immediate, but the surrounding vicinity at large. Not good. No blue rivulets in sight, only some vague bits of hope in the drainages leading off to some distant valley where the brown lines crowded together into a tight V shape that dropped from the ridge away and away.

The Ol' Man sank to his knees. He'd learned a bit from Coyote Thunder Owl, but clearly not enough. As he looked to the sky a tear welled up in his eye. No, wait. That's just a drop of rain. Rain? While a bit addled a second then a third bit of irrefutable evidence fell as the humidity he'd been wading through these past few days reached some critical mass and got itself together enough to form up into a proper bit of rain. In less than a minute, the teaming puddle of humidity got together regarding the season's deplorable work conditions, formed a proper union and promptly went on strike.

In joyous relief the Ol' Man reached for his water bottle as the (recently formed) United Brotherhood of Fluid fell into line and began its mass exodus from the heavenly field of labor and returned promptly back to earth. Spreading his map wide he diverted their efforts into filling his water bottle on their way past. As a cup's worth accumulated he could stand it no longer and he snatched up the bottle and slugged it down. No cure, but sure relief. He funneled in another cup's worth before heading another mile or so to the Skyline that wove its way along and crossed his path.

Dipping his cook pot into a ditch he quickly filled it up and began to replenish his supply of water. He scooped and treated the rain, a few cups at a time, as it wound its way down this impromptu river. His belly soon full, his supply soon replenished, the Ol' Man couldn't believe his luck. As he was filling his pot and filtering the last bit to top off his supply he noted a presence over his shoulder. Lesson learned, the young man appeared once more at his side. He sat silently, with the same bit of a smile as last we saw him.

Seeing that smile, the ol' fella had a sinking feeling this bit of rain wasn't merely good luck. He secured his freshly filled water and shouldered his pack. Once more ready to travel he looked to the young feller expectantly. (And a bit sheepishly, truth be told.)

As they fell into step, Coyote Thunder Owl looked to the Ol' Man and smiled his teasing smile that held no more warmth than the winter sun.

"Next time...It won't rain."

Esbit Tabs-

If I gave you everything that I owned
and asked for nothing in return
Would you do the same for me as I would for you?
Or take me for a ride
and strip me of everything including my pride?
But spirit is something that no one destroys

Traffic, "The low spark of high-heeled boys"

Trail Magic is an odd thing.   It's most common on the Appalachian Trail, especially down south as the season's herd of Northbound thru-hike prospects travel along. Folks called trail angels, locals, former hikers, fellow hikers, church groups and a host of other characters stop by with free food, rides, drinks or even beer.   Sometimes it's spontaneous, one person simply extending a kindness to another. Every year as more folks learn of the trails and the people who hike them, more folks come out to do something nice for the hikers.   Or really, to do something nice for themselves.

Some expect to see a little magic; some free food, unexpected rides, or even an angel to stop by and help them out. Some expect to meet good people or see stunning beauty. Many get those things and it's common enough, so much so that some come to expect or even demand this treatment from the trail; that may be why they are offended when these gifts come with disagreeable wrapping or fail to appear. Perhaps the trail targets these folks to teach them a lesson.

But trail magic is quite real, and it comes in many forms.

I was out on a section from Springer to Hot Springs, a bit late in the season to catch the majority of folks, but being mid-June the trail was crowded enough with Scout troops, teachers and families enjoying the summer. On the AT you don't need a TV to hear the news, each traveler passes the word. The word the last few days involved the approach of a nasty storm likely to cause serious trouble for any folks out and about. As the weather takes on a slightly different urgency on the trail, news of bad weather often travels faster than an approaching storm.

Not far past Wallace Gap I reached a high enough spot I figured it was worth turning on the phone and checking in with my wife. It'd been a few days since my last call and, with the storm coming, who knew when the next shot would be. Even all the way back in Chicago she'd heard of the storm, a big one building up that threatened to pound most of the country. It was even wreaking havoc by her at that moment and was expected to arrive in the hills of North Carolina where I stood the following day. I ended our conversation not long after realizing that if I put in some miles that evening I had a shot at weathering the storm at an upcoming attraction; Nantahala Outdoor Center. The NOC was about 30 miles away, and though it was a bit after dinnertime I figured it was an even race to get there by tomorrow afternoon to weather the storm with beer, burgers and a view of the river.

About midmorning the view from Wayah Bald and the howling winds told me the race was on in earnest, as the mighty storm outpaced me, forming a still distant but angry looking grey slash across the sky. I passed a scout troop heading the other way on the descent who was hoping to sneak in the peak before retreating to the NOC by van. The storm brought an electricity to the air, a freshness to the wind, and a quickening to my step as I raced along. About a dozen or so miles from the NOC I figured it was time for a quick meal to power me through the last and most exiting leg of the race.

Cold Spring shelter nearly sucked all the pleasure out of the day. It was a nasty little hovel of a shelter, with a pile of garbage along with the mildly famous plane crash scraps. The water source is a muddy trickle passing through the garbage pile and pissing through the small camp. There was a pile of garbage off to one side, including several tight little bundles of backpacker trash, almost enough of them to make it look like we may be outpacing the local rabble rousers. I'm not sure what people think ridge runners and trail maintainers should do but it is not hauling out garbage, no matter how neatly you pile it or attempt to disguise it amongst the trash of other visitors.

As I filled my water bag I heard a dank cough from the depths of the equally dank shelter emitted from a dank smoking fellow huddled within. I walked up to the low slung, three sided shed and sat near the edge to prepare a meal, thus making acquaintance with a fairly rough ridden Floridian who was thru-hiking the trail.

He was having a tough go of it, an older fella who owned a small stucco business. To his vast credit he realized years in the trades and other lifestyle choices had wrecked his health. "I wanted to do something before I could do nothing..." he told me regarding his choice to hike. He'd never heard of the trail until a few weeks ago; he just did a little online research and came up north to hike. He pretty well geared up at Wally World to save money, and he was using bleach to purify his water and a cheap Esbit stove to cook. It didn't look promising but he did look determined. We discussed the storm and he showed me the pile of wood he'd laid up. He wouldn't make it to the NOC, he'd be too tired to get ready if he pushed one shelter closer, so he'd made the choice this morning to stay put and expend his waning energy on hunkering down. The dozen or so remaining miles were more than he could manage.

But his story quickly took a turn south, the only real camping item he purchased was an inflatable mattress for sleeping. It, along with his Tampa Bay Buccaneers jacket, were stolen from his tent when he was visiting the visitor center at Amicalola. "That's one hell of a way to get welcomed to the trail, huh? I keep looking for it on somebody's back, it was a nice jacket and I'll bet you it's on the trail."

"No, my friend, that I can guarantee isn't the case. Many parks have poachers who pick off gear, especially at popular sites where tourists have their guard down. People on the trail generally don't steal from each other, but watch your stuff when you're in town and never leave your pack. Even if there's nothing in there some fool may take it, hoping to get a few bucks at the pawn shop." That made more sense to him, and actually seemed to make him feel better about the trail in general as the conversation progressed.

"Give me a bowl." I told him. He handed me an empty cup, "That's what I'm using." I filled his cup with a heaping helping of bulgur, pinto bean and veggies. "I can't take your food" and I smiled. "My portions are a bit big, my friend, and this is real food; it fills you faster than you realize. Besides...I'll be eating a big juicy burger in a few hours while you're holed up here crappin' your pants." That got a good laugh and the last of his pride gave way to his obvious hunger.

He'd been eating oatmeal, Snickers and ramen. He'd saved his last packet of soup for the worst of the storm and a Snickers for the hike out. He wasn't confident he'd make it down the steep and punishing descent to the NOC in a day. I wasn't confident he would either. Fresh blowdowns can slow any hiker, and this fella could take days if the storm was bad.

I wasn't planning a resupply at NOC but I certainly could make one. I dug out my food bag and pulled out what was left. He was using Esbit Fuel to cook, just as I happened to be. He was saving his last tab to start a fire. I dug out what was left of that as well. I returned a pack of soup and a single tab back to my pack in case I didn't beat the storm, and laid the rest of the food and fuel on the floor of the shelter. I'm no angel, but there are certain rules a good traveler should follow, and this was simply the right thing to do.

He'd finished most of the food during our short conversation, I dumped my portion into my Ziploc container and took mine "to go" since it was still too hot for me to eat. "This is good, it's like real food, too!" I told him how to prepare the food I had left him and shouldered my pack. He looked up at me from the shelter as I prepared to go and gave me one of those truly sincere thanks that you rarely get in town. As I shook his hand I gripped it a bit firm and locked his gaze in mine, "This, my friend, is how the trail works. Welcome to it. And enjoy your hike."

It took a bit to shake the gloomy shelter and its occupant from my mind as I headed down the trail. Shelters are part of the AT, but not always a pleasant part. Most are nice, but a few, like that one, seem to take something away from the place. The AT is no pristine wilderness, but a nasty shelter still sticks out like a spray painted porta-crapper in an otherwise beautiful public city park. But as the wind picked up and the approaching storm could be seen through the trees all thoughts of humanity faded away as the mighty west wind reminded me of the thrilling race I was a part of.

I didn't even pause at Cable Gap and quickly hit the last downhill to NOC as a few baby clouds driven by the approaching storm were swept up and pushed away, crying briefly as they went by. Like they always seem to, the last few miles dragged along as I expected to see the famous river rat trap appear around each bend or dip. The sky darkened to twilight as a monster crept up and loomed over my left shoulder and spit at me. But just after 2:00 I broke suddenly onto the long expected road and shot across it to secure a room for the night.

I had just enough time to lock in a room and shoot across the street to the outfitter when I suddenly hung a hard left and went to the bar instead. As I neared the porch the storm arrived in full force, soaking me as I walked the last few steps. I ordered a Newcastle and settled into a seat by the window as I watched the many visitors of the compound scramble in futility to reach cover. I sipped my beer as the lights flickered on and off, content with my choice of food and drink over casing the shelves of the outfitter while weathering the storm. Thankfully the intermittent power outages were not enough to hinder the tap system significantly.

Eventually I made my way to the outfitter for my resupply and to find some fuel. The NOC is a popular spot and a world-famous outfitter, so I expected a wide array of treats to choose from. I was soon to be disappointed. This late in the season the swarming herd of hikers had stripped the place clean and there was little to be had. I wandered upstairs to the stove section for my Esbit tabs but couldn't find them. I began to fear the worst. I headed back to the register, thinking perhaps such a common item would be kept near at hand by the counter.

An employee was wrangled up to help me out, and we headed back upstairs. He checked where I had just been then shook his head and went back to check the stockroom. I drifted around to check out the wares but began to think the fella had forgotten the smelly drunk in search of some fuel. As I was about to give up he returned empty handed. "Are you dry?" he asked. I nodded the affirmative and made a puzzled face as I debated what another 160+ miles of trail with no fuel might mean for me. He walked over to the stoves and began to dig through the boxes, finding a few Esbit brand boxes he opened the first and discovered it empty. Opening the next he took the six tabs that came with the stove and handed them to me. "This is it, no charge." Are you sure? I'll be happy to pay. "We should never be out of these, especially for a hiker. I'm one of the managers here, I'm sure this is the right thing to do."

So I cobbled enough food together to replace what I had given away. And just as it had that morning, the world's supply of available Esbit tabs was exchanged from one generous hand to one with a greater need; a circle of strangers briefly meeting at just the right time for just the right reasons. Because, my friends, just as a fella we all know and love had mentioned earlier in the day, "This is how the trail works."

I was up at 7:00 to pack up and get ready to go after a good breakfast. Leaving my pack in the bunkhouse, I headed down to the River's End Restaurant to wait for them to open up at 8:00 and eventually took my seat. As I sat and watched the results of the storm on the weather channel I noted the blurb across the bottom of the screen announcing that parts of Shenandoah had been shut down. Tough news for this season's Northbounders who had already faced Sandy during this tempestuous storm season on the trail. I would later learn that parts of the Smokies were also shut down for a short time and the storm was not as kind there, forcing a hiker to be helicoptered out with a compound fracture. I hoped the already beleaguered hikers up north had fared better.

Across from me one of the many Scout troops I had encountered were in for a weekend of rafting to conclude their trip here and celebrate earning their backpacking merit badge. As an Eagle Scout I am always encouraged to see scouts not only out, but out doing such life changing trips as a week on the AT. I silently raised a glass to all the fathers who give up their precious vacation time to take young boys out to become men. These are often fathers who are only there, "for the boys" and have little desire or interest in backpacking, making their efforts all the more inspiring. I had encountered this group around Wayah Bald and we each exchanged a friendly nod.

Not long into the meal another hiker joined them. He had suffered some sort of heat illness and the troop had given him some aid while they were out. They had left him at a shelter to recover, but were reunited here by chance so he could share his tale with the Scouts. After parting he had tried to leave the shelter, convinced he needed help. With his eyes on his feet he managed to shuffle another few miles in a bit of a delirium until he encountered a gravel road.

Suddenly, his feverish mind no longer knew what to do as this simple obstacle to his one foot in front of the other strategy was thwarted. He stood with his head down for some time, before hearing a voice, "Do Ya'll need a ride to town?" An old man was leaning on his car not twenty feet away on the gravel road. One of the Scout dads was leading the interview and asked the hiker what he would have done if the car had not come, "I don't know, but I was done. It was over for me and I was on empty."

At that I looked up and saw a familiar look, the look of a man who had reached his limit and faced it in the woods. Regardless of whether he was in a truly life threatening situation or not, he thought he was, and his mind had reviewed the possibility that there was no phone, no help. It was just him, the woods, and the end of the trail. His cup was not just empty, it was drained. My heart went out to this man as he struggled to explain the unexplainable.

I looked over at the inquisitor and saw another familiar look. One of the fathers replied, "Real lucky for you then he showed up huh?" in the conversational tone of a city fella who didn't understand exactly what happened. They rehashed his trip to town, the stop at the clinic, reviewed the skepticism regarding the appearance of the savior who according to the hiker, "Was retired with nothing better to do, and figured he'd help out the hikers even if he couldn't hike anymore himself." My heart went out to that well-meaning Scout leader, who just couldn't wrap his soul around the story being shared, and part of my mind drifted off in regret.

It's nice to get an unexpected ride, a cold drink, a free meal. It sure feels special when it happens, and I suppose I can understand that when you hear the "trail magic" stories you may begin to expect something special to happen to you. It likely will. And if something in you makes you doubt the whole concept and makes you un-comfy, no hard feelings. The trail won't go door to door drumming up converts, if you want it to leave you alone, it likely will.

But be careful how you define special. By town standards a lot of really special things happen on the trail. But by trail standards...often enough the definition of special is a bit closer to the true meaning of the word. The trail can twist you up a bit, make you think you're special, that great forces are bending the world your way. It will make you forget your place, encourage you to feel entitled to something. It will reward shallow expectations with equally shallow rewards. It will reinforce doubt with indifference.

Personally, I've never been to a hiker feed or seen one. I've been given two beers by strangers on the trail, neither of them on the AT. I once had a warm pop from a forgotten cooler. The closest thing I had to an angel giving me a meal was some drunk Chicagoan's playing hunter along the River to River Trail. I have never Yogi'd a thing or made the attempt. I once found a plastic bag of rotten oranges hanging from a tree, I packed it out. I've used the water cooler put there by the kind folks that live just north of Shenandoah. But I can claim to have experienced very little of the trail magic most folks commonly enjoy.

Not that I would snub my nose, mind you, I suppose it's just not the way the trail works for me.

I collected my check and paid up. As I walked across the trail, I stepped off onto one of the observation platforms over the river and watched the mist dance above the whitewater of the Nantahala. I considered the close of the conversation I had just heard as the dad finally pushed aside enough of his skepticism to generously offer, "Well either way, that was especially lucky for you that guy was there." The hiker looked off in the distance and I saw another look I recognized when events exceed the bounds of coincidence; a small, grateful smile. "Yes... it was something special."

I shed a few tears into the river and stepped back onto the trail. It's easy to get preachy, to have doubt, to seek the words for things you can't explain. Or try to explain what can only be felt. Sometimes it's best to smile to yourself and be content with what you're given.

From the outside looking in, I'd had a chance to observe a conversation I'd been in a few times before. I was gently reminded that the trail needed no deeper meaning or explanation. Some things can't be explained, or can only be done so with certain code words that have meaning only to a few.

As I gathered my pack from the bunkhouse and hit the trail, once more, my mind repeated the socially accepted words that translate into the Language of the Heart and explained it all to those who know the true meaning of, "It was something special."

Recycling-

Yvon- "The hardest thing in the world is to simplify your life, it's so easy to make it complex. What's important is leading an examined life because most of the damage caused by humans, is caused unintentionally, I think."

Doug- "And... In response to people saying "You can't go back." What happens if you get to the cliff, and you take one step forward, or you do a 180 degree turn, and take one step forward?

Which way are you going?

And which is progress?"

Doug Tompkins, Founder of: The North Face
Yvon Chouinard, Founder of: Patagonia
In conversation, "180 degrees South" a film by Chris Malloy

"Well ain't this a dump"

Ol'Man Willy was walking along with his pals; Coyote Thunder Owl and a young fella by the name of Red. And as correctly stated, the land they currently traversed was a wasteland. The trio was out wandering a section of foothills along no particular route, just a bit of tramping to see what they could see.

No trees grew, nor did any birds chirp, not even a mosquito wandered by. A few scrubby weeds had taken a tenuous hold here and there but all in all it was not a chunk of land high on anyone's list to visit. They were nearing the end of the trip and Coyote Thunder Owl had led them up a tricky little stretch to enter this valley to cut across it on their way out. Supplies were tight and the ol' fella and his younger pal were engaged in a bit of a debate on the subject to pass the weary miles.

Young Red was filled with the optimism of youth, and offered various options to extend limited resources, conserve what was in use, and reduce what was taken. More idealistic than practical the Ol' Man argued, "Take a sheet of paper for example. Ain't no way to make paper without taking a tree. Now running outta trees a foolish man may give up on getting more paper. But a clever man can shred up that old paper and make it new again, maybe even plant a tree in the meantime if he was truly trig. But short of that, a man's still gotta have some paper and there ain't no two ways about it."

Red was undeterred, "But when the clever man's son comes around he must bleach out his father's ink. He needs chemicals, energy, and resources to do this and make more paper. And even if his trig pappy plants that tree, the chemicals and smoke from his factory are bound to kill it before his son can benefit. No, there must be another way, for even that solution is only another temporary one for sure."

This bit went round and round for some time, as conversations tend to when blank miles of trail lie between a traveler and his rest. Finally the Ol' Man turned to Coyote Thunder Owl, not so much because he wanted an answer mind you, but more to break up the monotony of the conversation. "Well, it's up to you to settle the debate then fella, what does the wise man say on the subject."

After a bit of walking, truthfully a long enough bit to wonder if the query had been heard, the man so addressed got around to speaking. But as this was often his way, the pause did not bring overmuch discomfort to his companions. And as was his way, he answered directly. "Sometimes, there isn't enough to go around."

With the conversation more or less killed, the companions travelled on in silence. Coyote Thunder Owl led them to what could faintly be discerned as an old river bed long since dried up. As they followed its faint path it became a bit clearer, and off in the distance they noted a few scrubby shrubs which they set out for. Not only were foodstuffs in short supply, but water had long since run out as well. The old craft of their leader brought them to this place, where a deep dirty hole was all that remained.

Disappointment showed on every face, but there was little relief in making faces, so they set about to dig out the hole a bit.

Using a spare bit of cloth and some towels they wrung a bit of filthy water from the hole that exhibited a cloudy countenance and foul temperament. "This water is in need of a good bath" remarked the Ol' Man glumly. It was in bad enough shape that they chose to boil what little they could gather and took a rest from the noon sun to conserve their meager supply.

It was decided it was time for a meal as well, their last as it so happened. Upon careful examination of the remaining food it appeared that only Red and Coyote Thunder Owl had a meal each remaining. Three fellas and two meals.

"We'll divvy it up three ways, that is the fair way to do it." Said Red.

"We'll water it down, add some spices, and make a soup. That way we all get a full belly if not a full meal." Proposed the clever Ol' Man.

"Sometimes, there isn't enough to go around. One of us cannot eat. I insist it be me."

And that was that. Coyote Thunder Owl went back to the mud hole and attempted to squeeze out a few more drops while the others prepared their meal. Now truth be told, the other two were not all that happy with this arrangement, but once words were spoken they were rarely taken back by their friend. As they finished up preparing their meal, a scraggly looking fellow quite impossibly emerged from the bushes.

Addressing Red and the Ol' Man he introduced himself, "Ah, my good friends, I couldn't help overhearing your problem and thought I would offer my services to you if you were interested. For though I am a stranger, the Great Spirit has given me strong medicine. Good for problems such as this." While he was certainly scraggly, there was something to him. A dignity in his look and posture, some power in his weather worn features. Ignoring the improbable appearance of this fellow in this desolated land, or perhaps bewildered by it, the two looked at each other and Red spoke up first.

"Well, it's a pleasure to meet you sir, our friend has taught me to be kind to our fellow travelers, especially those who live the old ways as you appear to."

Ol' Man Willy nodded in assent of young Red's words, "Yar, a bit and a bit he has, I must admit that we do indeed have a problem. Although Coyote Thunder Owl has told me before that an old traveler is not always quite what he seems. But, be welcome here..." he said as he waved him in to sit down, "... what is your plan?"

Just then Coyote Thunder Owl returned from the water hole with a few more bottles of water and took notice of the new arrival. The strange fella unhappily took notice, but shared a cheery greeting anyway as it became clear to Red and the Ol' Man the two had met before. In response; a simple, respectful, nod of Coyote Thunder Owl's head was returned with the equally respectfully response, as he called the traveler by name, "Sinkalip." A name that drew a frustrated breath from the stranger.

"Now then...well... it is good to see you anyway as I say. And if it is alright with you, I had a proposal I was in the midst of proposing when you sauntered into camp, if you would be so kind as to allow me to lend my assistance. For before you had but two meals, and three hungry fellas. And now you have four empty bellies before the dinner pot and only the medicine of Sinkalip to help you."

"I have chosen not to eat, so the food that remains, and what is to be done with it, is the choice of these two here. I will remain out of the vote and refrain from speaking on that which no longer concerns me. The water will remain with me, for there is little to spare or chance on your power."

"An agreement as fair as the speaker and wise beyond your years old friend. And, so then, my new friends. Shall you let me help you with this problem so that we may all walk away full. I have great power, and this little bit of making a meal larger is little trouble if you will allow."

Now the remaining two were already guaranteed a meal, and their friend had already generously abstained. But the two felt a bit guilty to be sure. Red, secretly in his heart of hearts, believed in the old ways and medicine of the land. He was excited to meet this fellow, perhaps even have the chance to witness the old ways in person. He quickly agreed. The Ol' Man knew enough to doubt such silliness, but there was a practical bit of tradition at hand.

This kitchen sink fella had entered their camp, and they had no hospitality to extend, which in his book was a poor bit of manners at the very least. More accurately, he had eaten more meals thus far than he had the right, and the meal that his friend was passing up was long past stowed in his belly. He was pretty sure his friend had an accurate count on that score as well, and that made him feel downright shameful. So with a certain grudging hope that all could be made right, he too gave his permission to the stranger.

"That is very wise, for my power is great. So great in fact that it takes much of my energy. So, to take two and make four, I must first of course take the two meals before us. I will also need your spare cooking pot. For once I have eaten these two meals, I will have enough energy in my belly to create four meals and fill both pots to the brim. Then my friends, even Coyote Thunder Owl will eat his fill."

So Sinkalip sat down before them and gobbled up the remaining food. Then he looked at both of them solemnly and said, "And now, I must gather my medicine and prepare. Wash out this pot good, put it with the other in the bush over there. When my medicine is ready, I will go to the bush. With a great thunder you will hear my power work. And the pots will be full. Let me prepare." Sinkalip sang a song in a strange language and swayed around for some time. And then he entered a deep meditation.

Red watched in awe. The Ol' Man was fairly certain Sinkalip had fallen asleep.

Finally, after the heat of the afternoon had passed, Sinkalip began to stir. A small gurgle escaped his belly, and he smiled at his two friends, "Ho-ha! Hoka Hey! My medicine is ready, I can feel my belly filled with it." The two stirred from their own naps and looked at the strange fellow as he hopped about. "Once more I honor the Great Spirit by using my power as he intended! Make way, I will go to the bush and you will see the power of Sinkalip!"

He rushed to the bushes and arranged the pots. And indeed a great noise was heard, a mighty grunt and a thunderous eruption! Another grunt and a great noise came from the bush. And then some more grunts. A great passing of wind and a low rumble. Some type of struggle went on as the last of his medicine must have been forced from his body. Finally, slightly weary looking, Sinkalip emerged from the bush with two heavy pots in his hand, pausing to address them before fully entering the camp.

"My medicine did not fail me, although it was a mighty struggle to fill the second pot. Alas, I have only managed to fill it three-quarters full. But fear not. Using my medicine is sustenance enough for my old bones. And so, I will leave all of this to you three to split up. Enough to fill three bellies, and my satisfaction must be in a job well done, my reward in using my power as the Great Spirit intended. I will leave you to it in peace and accept no thanks for the gift of my power."

In stunned silence Ol' Man Willy and Red watched as Sinkalip struggled to carry the two pots over to them. They were clearly filled, a true miracle like the ones Coyote Thunder Owl occasionally told of in his stories from the time long past when powerful beings like this one travelled the land. Staring at Sinkalip as he passed them, they took little notice of the pots as he set them down and bid them farewell. They watched in awe for some time as he walked from the camp.

Finally the lure of the pot could be ignored no longer. Red dug in without looking down and shoveled a spoonful into his mouth. The Ol' Man looked down just in time betrayed by his nose he more closely examined the loose gruel in his pot.

"Shit! He's eaten our food and shit in our pots!" He stood up and tossed the full pot in futility at the retreating stranger and shouted, "What power is this you scoundrel!"

A faint laugh returned from the now distant Sinkalip,

"My clever friend...you town folk's call it Recycling!"

No Regrets-

After a bit of adventure around and about the Denver area, my visit with my father would culminate in a bit of a road trip down to Mesa Verde. To see the winter delights and sights for certain, but mainly to spend some time together on the road. Down we headed to Wolf Creek Pass and over towards the lovely trail town of Pagosa Springs. We made a brief but quickly aborted attempt to hike into a remote hot springs on the west side of the pass. But wading near waist deep snow even with snowshoes on proved to be a tricky bit of work for this writer, not to mention his more aged father.

I was a bit disappointed at this aborted effort to partake of the hot springs that I so love, so as a consolation prize my father generously agreed to spring for a stay at the resort in the center of town that boasted dozens of naturally fed hot springs located picturesquely on the river that flowed through town. The rooms weren't at all worth the price paid, but when balanced against the tubs themselves it was a fair deal in my opinion that would prove to be a true bargain when all was said and done.

My dad is not quite the hot tub fiend that I am, so it took him a bit longer than the approximately ninety seconds I spent unceremoniously tossing down my bag and changing into a suit after our long day of travel. I was immersed in blissful warmth and quite satisfied when my pappy joined me twenty minutes later. We drifted from pool to pool, each with a slightly different view, temperature, and vibe. He didn't attempt the Lobster Pot but did gamely brave the tub that sat directly in the San Juan itself; as close as one can get to the remote pool we had attempted to reach without tramping miles through waist deep snow.

As the warmer waters of the upper tubs mingled with the snowmelt we sat directly on the riverbed and unwound from our day. Pretty women are to be found all over this great land, but outdoorsy towns, particularly out west, seem to conjure up the rare breed of natural, confident, and pretty as the Mother Earth herself beauties that I am so fond of. A tall, lean, long haired brunette of the species was making a similar circuit of the pools this fine day. Any makeup other than the slowly setting winter sun and soft blush of spring fed warmth worn on her cheeks would have marred her natural perfection.

Now my pappy may not be the finest companion for breaking trail to reach a remote spring, or have the heat tolerance for the hours long soaking of a true springs aficionado, but he did have a skill that always comes in handy. My father is a talker, and while some may argue I've picked up a bit of this skill in regards to the written word; in face to face matters my father is still by far my superior.

After a brief period in the river tub my father had excused himself to the room for a bit. I lost myself in the river. The distant peaks, quaint mountain town and gradually lowering sun all conspired to make me utterly happy. Rather than turned off by the rapidly switching temperature that had driven my father from this creekside tub, I was exhilarated by the occasional switches from hot spring to near frozen snow melt as this loosely formed tub of piled rocks changed its character as often as the river surface dancing nearby.

Eventually I returned to the human world and worked my way back up to the rest of the tubs to find my pappy. Who was busily soaking his calves next to the aforementioned western willow of stunning beauty, engaged in gregarious conversation and exercising his natural talents to their fullest. No shoddy wingman is my father; immediately waving me over to meet the mountain maiden and make her acquaintance.

Now rather than picturing some creep, picture instead an average looking fellow, of average height, looks, and weight. Now imagine that this fellow is as in love with meeting folks as I am with meeting trees and you will simply see him for a fella who loves conversation. He good naturedly flirts shamelessly with most women, young, old, attractive or hideous. A trait my brother and I found embarrassing when younger but with a few more miles under my hipbelt I began to appreciate it as the simple love of the traveler interested in walking the trails of friendship whenever possible. He could joke with a fella, flirt with a lass, and shamelessly wink at your grandmother; a gentleman and a rascal. And while not everyone is up for his talents, for those that are, he's good company.

Playing matchmaker and attempting to proceed with his long standing plan of getting his first born to follow him out west he kept our new friend interested in our conversation. Both of us being of marriageable age and unspoken for as it would turn out it came as little surprise that after an hour of soaking up the heat he proposed our new friend join us for diner. Quick plans were made, and now that his favorite pastime lay around the bend, he changed and dressed for the next activity on the docket with a speed that easily surpassed his son.

Dinner was a stunning success. Beauty is as fast fleeting as a sunset, no matter how stunning. Intelligence, wit, kindness, sincerity, confidence; all the truly lasting and worthwhile qualities worth pursuing emerged in the lady. This willow stood tall with an inner beauty and grace that was far more intriguing than any other visible asset she bountifully possessed at the waterside earlier in the day. It was the perfect traveler's meal; conversation, cheer, companionship and enough intrigue to fill us all.

The admiring stares at our companion by the waiters and busboys began to give way to the looks that imply more clearly than the clock that the restaurant is nearing close. So my father kindly paid as promised and we headed out. Work called to our friend in the morning and signaled a regretful end to the weekday evening for all involved. My father deftly drifted off as my new friend and I exchanged some contact information and a warm hug. While sparks and fireworks are the ending most men hope for when encountering a lady like this, my preference is the low coals of a true fire when the prospect of a longer stay than a night is hoped for.

My father and I said goodbye and took a short stroll around the compact downtown area to stretch our legs and bellies after the lengthy meal. He once more made a case, harder to refute after the evenings dinner, of the fine scenes, nature, and inhabitants awaiting me should I make the move across country to follow him. After a bit of wandering for a while now, perhaps it was time to settle in a place that offered such a fine balance of work, play, nature, and companionable folks.

It was a mildly chilly December night and the town not too large so we found ourselves back at the resort in relatively short order. It had been a long day to be sure, and another lay ahead tomorrow. While my father chose a bit of reading to wind down from the evenings excitement I choose instead to take advantage of the unique feature of the resort; for guests and members, the pools were open all night long. While some prefer a cold shower, I find a deep hot soak to be a better relaxant. The night was clear, the air cold and crisp. A soak under the spectacle of the billions of distant burning suns in warm waters was too good to pass up.

As luck would have it, I was not the only one who had such plans. After a good half hour to myself a couple drifted into the resort. They spent some time apart before inviting me over to join them and share a beer or three from the cooler they had brought down. Like my father I enjoy meeting folks as well, while not quite so skilled or bold to invite myself over, I rarely turn down the invitation once made. So I joined this couple in the appropriately named Sunset Social Club Pool for a beer, a soak, and a chat.

Finding a woman as good as our dinner companion is a challenge for any outdoorsman, as is finding a fine place to settle down. A subject my pappy so often angled at as he believed he had found such a place. But invariably the true challenge rears its head; how to make a living in such a place.

It was this problem I had been pondering under the stars as I stewed in the Lobster Pot a few minutes ago. This couple seemed to have found a solution I was interested in as the initial chit-chat led to the discussion of profession. They were general contractors who travelled around doing retail build-outs for a couple of well-known chains. The work was tough, with tight deadlines and travel. But they could manage it working only about half the year onsite. The rest of the time they returned, quite profitably, to their home here in town.

They fondly described the seasonal rhythms of the mountain town outdoors scene; winter skiing, spring rafting, summer biking and fall hiking. Easily balanced with their work assignments lasting a few weeks of around the clock construction to open retail stores as quickly as possible for their clients. As they worked wherever, they could live wherever, as did their crew who simply met them at the job and went home when it was done. It sounded like a fine way to solve the tricky problem so often encountered by the outdoors folk who must choose between poverty in paradise, or stability in town.

They were good folks, with the general ease and openness often found on the trail among travelers. The altitude, the springs, the beers, and the evening all added to the slight giddiness I felt creeping in. As it turned out I was not the only one having more fun than one ought to be having. Quick to laugh, quick to friendship, this couple in their early forties slipped quite quickly into that familiar companionship and camaraderie so common to the outdoors folks I find myself in company with whenever I travel.

In fact, as the evening wore on a few gears in my brain finally made the connection that this woman looked eerily similar to a certain married woman whom I had encountered not too far back on life's trail in the fine state of Vermont. So much so that I had to force logic and common sense to prevent me from asking if she was indeed the same woman. That nagging mystery solved, I was able to refocus my brain on another development that should have been obvious to someone who had encountered this species of tub dweller before.

While I wasn't specifically in their home, they were not directly offering their hospitality to me in the same fashion, the clear fact emerged; I once more found myself in the company of swingers. Sharing beer, easy companionship, common interest and good conversation had clouded my perception but once more I had found myself in their company. Once more, they proceeded with surprising directness to the heart of the matter when the time came.

I have found that the trail is often cyclical in nature. That experiences tend to repeat until resolved. While no grand realization unique to my personal experience, all cliché's have some basis in fact. Last time this encounter occurred I was shocked into inaction by the boldness and suddenness of the encounter.

This time a more natural drifting approach and an opening offer of a massage gently guided me. Rather than vague words coupled with a physically direct call to action, a more subtle physical invitation and little doubt as to the planned course of action proceeded. In short, my mission, should I choose to accept it, was quite clear, required little immediate decision and plenty of time to warm up to the idea.

While history repeats itself, it is rare one gets a chance to relive such a specific bit of history one regrets. This time there were none.

This is no cheap dime store romance novel, so I'll spare those details which would be ungentlemanly to share. The whole affair was oddly comfortable, familiar, and a bit lazier than one might expect. Travelers often find themselves sharing emotional intimacy with ease, while I should not have been, I was surprised to find that physical intimacy flowed quite as easily when the evening's campfire companions are willing.

Now I'm no porn star, and this was no porno. It wasn't all sunshine, rainbows and unicorn screams of ecstasy. It's a bit awkward to perform in a public space, with an audience, and from the depths of a steaming body of water. Little of the scintillating details you may expect occurred, but with a general pleased feeling all around, it ended well enough for all concerned. It was an experience I have yet to repeat. But the trail led me here again, and this time it seemed wrong to take a blue blaze when the trail so clearly went towards this encounter.

In part because I'd felt I'd missed out on something in Vermont, some school boy fantasy or dear Penthouse experience that all American males seem to crave. In part because I had regrets. In part because, well, why not?

One travels for adventure, to be put out of your comfort zone, to have a tale to tell when one returns. To leave yourself behind once in a while. And sometimes because the trail is kind enough to lead you where you need to go if you're bold enough to follow. It turned out to be a good section. A bit of trail that satisfied an itch I had to scratch before I knew it didn't need to be repeated, and I was glad I didn't miss out.

The next morning we headed out to Mesa Verde. It was a shocking sight for this Midwestern resident to be sure. The vastness of the park, clearly visible for miles as we drove on the winding roads to its center.

My father and I were a bit anxious and regretful. The hour was late and we greatly feared we'd have little chance to see the park. As we wound our way in we ducked into passing attractions and excavation sites, doing the quick, car-touring, cram it all in American park visitor routine.

As we wound to main visitor center we thought we ducked in to find out the bad news. We figured we'd be shortly kicked out as the sun set and the park was likely to close. We had only this day before we had to turn back towards Denver. We had overreached trying to get the grand tour, checking off all the sites in our whirlwind. We'd debated a bit even coming out as we knew time was short. But as usual, the trail snuck up from behind.

It turned out, we were a bit early in fact, according to the ranger. This was a bit confussing. It was quite crowded in fact considering the late hour, winter season, and remoteness of the park. Like the couple the night before, everyone here seemed to know something was going to happen that we weren't planning on.

We shrugged our shoulders and followed the flow out the back door. Perhaps we'd stumbled upon some ranger led stargazing tour, the trail looked like it wound out to one of the overlooks. Likely a fine open platform with a vast view of the sprawling maze of cuts from the plateau and the sky above.

But as we turned a corner, it was not the stars above, but those below that drew us up short. Thousands of paper bags with tea candles in them lined each side of a long winding trail that led down to one of the famous settlements cut into the cliff. The cliff dwellings below were also lit up by gentle candlelight. Even without this prime attraction just the sight of the candlelit trail winding down would have been stunning enough.

The Luminaria Holiday. Once a year, for one night, the park is set up like this. We had never heard of it. It was amazing to see, and unlike many park service special programs or tours, nothing cheap, cheesy, or touristy about it. The candlelight was just the right thing to show off this stunning park. I won't do the park, myself or the reader any further disservice by attempting to put it into words. If you have the opportunity, you may stop by one day and make the attempt yourself if you like.

As I write this tale, years down the trail later; one notes how recollection is weighted by the lasting import of the experience had. As shown by the words of this tale and the quantity assigned to each. An author's subconscious accident I note as I review the tale in final editing.

Serendipity is an uncommon word, used with regularity by many a hiker.

I have a general good feeling of fond adventure with my father, my oldest friend and travel companion. A very sharp image of Mesa Verde during the Luminaria and the deep sense of peace when I entered the darkness of the kiva, alone despite the crowd; as the candles mysteriously blew out when I sat quietly within the Earth. Of things so special they can't be written even by someone as brutally shameless as myself.

I have only the vaguest notion of the carnal pleasures of the hot tub, the view of the mountains in the distance as I sat in the river bottom tub form more clearly in my mind. Despite being the only ménage a trois I will likely partake of in this life, the pleasure of the warm hug shared with the good mountain woman stands out as the greatest physical pleasure of the trip. Our dinner, my wingman, and the pleasant waters of the springs the more memorable events of that evening by far.

Clearest of all though, the great kindness of the trail stands out. The mysterious way it winds to correct itself when least expected. How adventure is nearly always met with reward and one tends to arrive at the perfect place at the perfect time. The opportunity to try being something else, in order to fully appreciate the person you actually are. The trail always leads to the right place, wither you knew it or not.

While misfortune, missed opportunity, hardship, and occasional regret may darken the path: these things tend to work themselves out, often forgotten in the brilliance of the next bright spot. I cannot guarantee the same for you, or even that every trip taken has gone so well. But given the chance to step back, and look back on the trail as a whole. I have no regrets.

The End of the Book-

To the East:
Two Trees-

It is not easy to dwell always in the presence of God and not feel the power of His goodness. I have attended church-sarvice in the garrisons, and tried hard, as becomes a true soldier, to join in the prayers; for, though no enlisted sarvant of the king, I fight his battles and sarve his cause, and so I have endeavored to worship garrison-fashion, but never could raise within me the solemn feelings and true affection that I feel when alone with God in the forest.

There I seem to stand face to face with my Master; all around me is fresh and beautiful, as it came from His hand; and there is no nicety or doctrine to chill the feelings. No no; the woods are the true temple after all, for there the thoughts are free to mount higher even than the clouds.

James Fenimore Cooper- Pathfinder; or the Inland Sea.

Though I am no expert on trees I know enough to know that in layman's terms there are basically two types; coniferous, or evergreen, which do not lose their leaves and deciduous; whose leaves do fall. Before anyone feels compelled to muck this up with scientific fact I fully admit there is more to it than that but the basic classification will suffice for this tale.

In my front yard sit two trees. One is a pin oak, a regal tree that despite being deciduous doesn't drop its leaves when the weather turns cold. The other is a flowing bald cypress, an evergreen whose needles turn brown and blanket my yard every autumn. Each morning when I back out my truck from under their branches I see them both through my windshield during the momentary pause needed to put the truck in drive before beginning my day.

Science has skirted this contradiction by calling the cypress a "deciduous conifer", an oxymoronic evergreen that is not evergreen and drops its needles. Although hard to see, the squirrel family in the yard call the pin oak home. That fact that its leaves do not fall in winter makes the tree an excellent source of prime building material. Allowing the family who lives there a year round supply of fresh insulation for their nest and a healthy crop of little ones each spring.

These trees remind me of one of nature's simplest lessons; there are no absolutes in nature. Just like the evergreen that turns brown or the oak that retains its leaves it is not nature, but only man, who wants to see things in black and white. While the two leggeds of the world can make their attempts at order and classification the standing ones in my yard and the little four legged family who live there gently laugh at us each morning at our silliness.

There are several Good Books, if truth be told. Many fine scientific papers, journals and discoveries published every year. Copies of these books do not arrive mysteriously one day in the hands of man, nor has science yet figured out how to make a transportation replicator to beam their publications to us. At the end of the day, these great works are simply printed on the carcass of a tree, likely a conifer. A simple tree; killed, shredded, pulped and pressed into paper to carry the thoughts of one two legged to another.

Do not misunderstand; both science and religion are of great value to us all. But likely so was the tree they were printed on to the hand that made it. Ironically, these words are likely to be printed on such a medium. Although science has a bit of the facts sorted out; unlike any of our great works, the tree does appear mysteriously. No human required. Divine intervention if such a notion is to be believed.

What makes us unique is that we can choose what we each believe is right and wrong, but those are simply beliefs, not facts. The absoluteness of science or religion is often colored grey by the world around us.

If you choose to believe that there is a fella who owns the place, take a hard look at the place he made while you debate the subject. More often than not I find not black, white, or grey; but every color and possibility in that creation.

You believe in the blessed prairies, and I have faith in the sayings of my fathers. If both are true, our parting will be final; but if it should prove, that the same meaning is hid under different words, we shall yet stand together, Pawnee, before the face of your Wahcondah, who will then be no other than my God. There is much to be said in favour of both religions, for each seems suited to its own people, and no doubt it was so intended.

James Fenimore Cooper- The Prairie

To the South:
Sinkalip-

As the shit filled pot flew from the hand of Ol' Man Willy the contents of its twin was hastily spewed forth from the mouth of Red. Coyote Thunder Owl offered the water to the horrified and spluttering Red. After Sinkalip's parting words drifted by he smiled his non-smile at the old man, "Sometimes...there is only enough for one."

"He's already gone and was never truly here..." Coyote Thunder Owl caught the arm of the Ol' Man as he was about to give chase to the distant form of Sinkalip. "The taste in my mouth is still here!" moaned Red, bringing a genuine smile to the face of Coyote Thunder Owl as he looked down on Red with some concern, "Rather, I should say, the fella you just supped with did not wear his true face, here he was, but never quite here if you take my meaning?"

"Can't say as I do," said the ol' fella as he snapped a twig from the shrub and handed it to Red, "better the taste of twigs than logs, eh lad?"

Ah, these were good and hearty travelers indeed. The smile of Red began to turn into a grin, and finally a good laugh was had by all over the encounter. With the worst of the sun's heat beginning to fade and there being no relief in this horrid place the trio gathered themselves up and began the march to escape the valley.

In truth is was a horrid place, and the situation quite desperate. They'd squeezed out perhaps a quart's worth of water a piece from the mud hole. Certainly not enough to sustain a march across friendly terrain, and it was a near thing indeed in such an unfriendly place.

Coyote Thunder Owl often told old tales around the evening's fire, or occasionally as they walked the land. Usually the walking tales and old medicine stories were light-hearted and brought a bounce to the step as they travelled along. But this was a grim march through a grim land, and merry words would not likely distract the mind and give freedom to the body. So Coyote Thunder Owl chose a tale to match the gravity of the land, with power enough to hold the minds of the trio in sway; so their bodies could concentrate all their efforts on the task at hand.

And so it began, "This land is known as The Valley of the First People....

Though few, if any pass through it any longer, and none have lived here for many years. I have told you the story of the naming day, when the Great Spirit gathered all the creatures and told them of the coming of the two legged, giving each of them a proper name to carry forth from that day. I have told you how The Trickster plotted to get a new name of great power, but arrived last after all the other names were chosen and spoke to the Great Spirit in his Lodge.

"Coyote, "said the Great Spirit, "You were meant to keep your name, so I made you sleep late. Your name suits you well, and I have much need of you when the first people come. I will give you many powers to help you, and you must go forth and make the valley where the people will live safe. You will be able to change your shape, talk to any being, and if you should be killed you will be brought back to life.

When the people arrive, you must be as chief to these new people, for they will arrive as babes, with no skill or knowledge. While all the other animals have good medicine and useful gifts, only you Coyote can use all medicines, teach the people of all the clans. So go forth and be a good chief and teacher, and when the first people have grown strong... Leave them be to flourish and return to me here at my lodge."

So Coyote rushed home to tell his wife of his new power, and left her alone in their lodge while he went to the Valley of the First People. The Great Spirit sent people from all the clans, and each of the other clan chiefs came to Coyote to give a great gift for the first people.

Buffalo brought a great hide, which was used to form the first tipi, and a great slab of meat to dry for the people. Eagle brought his best feathers, to bless the arrows of the first people, and taught them songs that could fly high enough to reach the Great Spirit. Bear brought his knowledge of all the plants and berries that were good to eat, and left stories to tell that would provide much wisdom to the new people.

Coyote took all these gifts and used them to prepare the way for the first people. When they arrived he shared these gifts, and many more, giving the people the fire that burned in his belly and the cunning that had so long served him well. Much to the wonder of the first people he did enter into great battles to clear the valley of the dark things that were there. He died many times, performed many feats, took many wives, and did many foolish things. But he was loved by the first people, who learned much from what he did right, and more from what he did wrong.

After a few generations all was well with the first people, and Coyote began to feel the pull to answer the Great Spirit's command. To leave them to flourish and return to his lodge. But Coyote grew bitter at the thought. Here he was a great chief, powerful, respected; all the things he had always wished for. And these people were great indeed, all because of him. The people did well, living in balance with all the other clans. Taking only when needed, caring for the land, and honoring all around them.

Because he did not want to leave, Coyote convinced himself he had more to teach. That not only was he a great chief of a great people, but the greatest chief of all the clan chiefs. He told the first people that they were the greatest of all the clans, and it was time to act that way. Coyote told them, "We will show the others that we are the chiefs of this land! We will need many arrows to hunt and fill our bellies."

And so Coyote called to all of the winged ones who lived in the valley, and demanded their feathers so the people could build arrows. "But without feathers we cannot fly, and we will die." protested the birds. "So be it!" shouted Coyote as he yelled his war cry and began to kill the birds to take what he wanted. Many winged ones fell that day, but Eagle came and led them away, "Return to the lodge of the Great Spirit Coyote!" were the parting words as Eagle led all the winged ones from the valley, never to return.

The people were proud, fat, and happy for several days as they ate the winged ones and fashioned many arrows. But soon the feast ended and their hunger arose. Coyote called to all the four legged of the valley, and demanded meat to feed the people. "But that is not the way it should be, if you kill us today, there will be no generation to feed you tomorrow." But once more Coyote led the people and fell upon the four legged and many were killed.

A great feast was had that went on for even longer, the people had never known such plenty. They proclaimed Coyote a great leader, themselves a great people. Coyote feasted and enjoyed the pleasures of many women in camp, but eventually even the great feast came to an end and once more the people were hungry. Coyote called to the Standing Ones, knowing that some of the smaller four legged escaped into their branches or hid in their roots. "Give up those hiding amongst you and we will spare you!" he demanded.

But the oldest of the Standing Ones laughed at Coyote, "Return to the Lodge of the Great Spirit, Coyote, we will not abandon those that call our limbs and toes their homes, all have a right to live in this valley, you fool, and you have tricked yourself and these people." Coyote was furious at the reminder of his old name, and burned all the trees to the ground, and the people made great digging sticks from the trunks and dug up all the roots.

The little food obtained from the last of the four legged did not last long. The furious work to gather the meal was little reward. The people thought on the words of the great chieftain of the trees and began to look differently at their great chief Coyote. But clever and quick as always he launched a plan for another feast. He called to the crawling ones, and the creeping ones... but they did not answer his call. So the people circled the great prairie that remained and started a great fire at the edges so that none could escape.

The people feasted on the snakes, lizards, and insects of the valley. Laughing to each other at the cleverness of their chief to have stopped Mosquito from ever biting them again. A good feast was had, these clans being more plentiful than even Coyote had realized. But eventually the people grew hungry again. With the forest burned, the prairies destroyed, only the steep slopes of the valley's rim had life to pursue. So Coyote led the people into the territory of Bear, and demanded he come out.

Bear laughed at Coyote, "You fool, leave this valley at once before all is lost. My people have eaten up all that is here to eat, chewed the seeds, spread and fertilized them so they may return next spring. It is autumn and we go to our long rest." Coyote shouted, "Then we will eat you, grub gobbler!" but Bear swept a mighty paw and knocked the chief to the ground, "I have sent my people away, If by spring we awaken and still find you here in this valley, I will take my people away with the same haste as Eagle."

And so, tired and hungry, the people returned to the valley. They began to look around and see wisdom in Bear's words. Winter was coming and they had done nothing but take and feast. The winged, the four legged, the standing ones, the crawling ones... nearly all the clans driven away or killed. The people lay in the center of the valley for many days near the river that split it, quenching their hunger by filling their bellies with its waters. They occasionally pulled a fish from the river, but not enough to satisfy them.

With none of the other clans around, the finned ones were quickly fading as well. So Coyote came up with a plan. He called to the people and they dug a great hole in the center of the valley next to the river. Then when all was ready, Coyote commanded the people to cut the wall between them and all the waters of the river rushed into the hole, leaving all the remaining finned ones flopping about for the people to gobble up.

With all of the Standing Ones killed no rains fell in the valley. With all of the crawling ones gone the waste of the people lay on the bare ground and made many sick. The stagnant pool of water made them sicker still and many died. Coyote gathered up the remainder of the tribe of the first people and began to walk to the edge of the valley. "The Great Spirit has many lands beyond this valley! He has hidden them from you, we will escape this trap and feast once more." So the people trudged on.

Coyote realized that the last of the clan chiefs had not been seen for some time, that the Buffalo Clan escaped the great hunt of the four legged. "Come forth shaggy one! My people are hungry and it is your duty to feed them." And before long Buffalo came to the people.

"It was the duty of the people to care for the prairies, so that my clan could grow strong and feed yours. You have failed to keep this bargain Coyote. The Great Spirit has sent me to beg of you to return to his lodge, and promised to spare the people. I give you my body, to feed the people while you make the journey. It is the command of the Great Spirit, and so it will be done."

And the great Clan Chief Buffalo laid his body down and he dropped his robes so the first people could sustain themselves. But even at this noble sacrifice the trickster was not deterred. "Ha! This fool has given us the means to leave this valley and take what the Great Spirit has hidden from us!" The people made a great feast of Buffalo while Coyote prepared.

He used the great bones of Buffalo to fashion a device, stretching the sinew between the bones, using levers and clever tricks. He made a seat from the skull and hide of Buffalo and many other clever inventions along the way. Finally after seven days, his great marvel was done.

"It has taken all my cunning and cleverness to create this wondrous invention, but it is done. Your great Chief Coyote has not failed you, for I have taken what the Great Spirit has given, foiled and outsmarted this plot against us. My medicine is greater! We can now leave this valley."

Coyote Thunder Owl had been talking for some time, night had fallen and they had reached the steep cliffs at the edge of the valley. He sang softly to the four winds, giving tobacco to each. He called humbly to those above, and those below. Finally he asked gently of the Great Spirit to see them safely from this valley. The three friends sat long at the foot of the cliffs, until after some time the hoot of a lone owl could be heard.

They followed its call. The way was treacherous, difficult, and potentially fatal. "A very near thing" as the Ol' Man liked to recall such mountaineering adventures that can easily turn out quite poorly for those who undertake them.

But call by call they found their way in the darkness. Groping along they left the valley, ascending a pass that even Coyote Thunder Owl would not have found. They safely reached the rim barricading the valley and descended to the far side. As the steep backside gave way to the plains below, they found a small stream and took water. A final hoot seemed to wish them well. The trio quickly fell asleep. The owl was never seen.

In the morning a small hill stood out in the surrounding plain. Coyote Thunder Owl led them to it and he sprinkled a little tobacco at its base before they began their climb. Once more he made a circle of tobacco, and the three sat down on the top in silence. Coyote Thunder Owl finished his story.

The First People lined up to depart the valley. Levers were pulled, sinew was stretched. As the first of the tribe sat in the empty skull of Buffalo, the people watching rejoiced at the power of their Chief. He pulled a final lever on his greatest contraption and the people cheered.

One by one they climbed into the invention of their Great Chief Coyote. They were flung into the air to soar as the winged ones, flying over the rim of the valley and escaping the constraints laid on them by the Great Spirit.

After the last person was sent from the valley, Coyote climbed into his contraption, proud at all he had achieved and built in this place. But he had grown too big for it, his people too great to be held back by the other clans. They had stood in his way, nearly defeated him, but in their last foolish plea he had found a way to prevail.

The Great Spirit had cheated his people, but Coyote had found a way to do what no other could. He pulled the lever and flew through the air. Not by the power given him, but only through his own cleverness and invention. "I will lead my people beyond the reach of even the Great Spirit!" he triumphantly declared as he flew through the air.

A few days later, the Great Spirit arrived. He jumped over the body of Coyote three times and brought him back to life. A great stench filled Coyote's nose as he returned to life and took in his surroundings. He was on a high spot in the great plain, and outside the valley as planned. He could see the plentiful land about him, but could not ignore the smell below.

His people were all dead. Heaped in a great pile of waste, flung here by his great invention. They were stinking and rotting in a great mound below him. Sitting next to him was the Great Spirit. "I didn't build that clan to fly." Said the Great Spirit with a wink. "That was quite clever indeed, you are always such a delight the way you create medicine that was never intended. But as always Coyote, you trick only yourself. Medicine is not yours to make, only to use. Once more you imitate others, with such folly as to imitate even me. And so well you begin to believe your imitation is real."

And the Great Spirit sighed, "These people are much like you my friend, achieving much; so much they forget the balance of things. Tricking themselves into believing they are not merely an imitator. I had hoped you would come back to my lodge, content with all the great power afforded you as Clan Chief to these new people. Happy in receiving the honor and praise you have so long hoped for. But perhaps I tricked myself as well."

"I will bring some new people, and you will be their chief. I will give them all the Earth, as I have given it to all of the other clans. The clans will not give all their gifts as freely, nor share their medicine until it is earned. You will be their chief once more. You will think I have taken all your power, but that is because you fool yourself. I will give you a great power."

"You will still be clan chief, though no people or clan will heed your command. You will be in charge of the growth of all things. In your frustration you will trick the people, teach them humility and the foolishness of their actions. You will keep them in balance, though you yourself will never find it. When the two legged get too clever you will be cleverer. When they seek to trick, you will trick them. When greed fills their heart, you will steal from the greedy. You will get no credit for these actions, you will be hated and feared. But always you will be respected, which was ever your greatest wish."

"You will still be brought back to life, you will still change your shape, and you will still speak any language. All your powers remain, but so do all your flaws and faults. Your belly will always be empty as punishment for you actions against the other clans. You will only scavenge or steal your food from the two legged. This will ensure you do the job I am sending you to do." With a wink and a smile, "For we both know how important keeping your belly full is to you."

The Great Spirit stood up to leave, "The two legged will be here once more. But I will spread them out in small groups so their tribes will be as nothing compared to the unity found amongst the other clans. They will have to fight and grow wise for many generations. Maybe one day they will unite and take their place in harmony, or maybe they will fail. There is no new place for them now, only the

Earth, as you wished. Do your job well Coyote, and perhaps this time you and the two legged clan will land in a better place."

Coyote Thunder Owl patted the mound beneath them. "We have walked the Valley of the First People, and now you sit on the results of their effort, and the end of our ancestors. The old languages are lost or dying, shifted, blended. The first tribes losing their identities. Who can say? But perhaps that is what the Great Spirit intends, for one people to speak one language.

However, in one of the languages, long ago, perhaps even before the first people came…. There was a name, which no one wanted.

Sinkalip. The Imitator. The Trickster. Coyote."

"You have met Sinkalip, head of our clan. He is a fool, and he is our chief. Remember him well, take note of him when he passes, learn what he teaches; and if you do this well… you will never meet him again. Now you know why Coyote must steal his food, and shit in our pot."

Let us leave these travelers now at this sad mound, and hope that none of our clan ever finds such a place again.

I have told you a story, as it was told to me.

Hoye wa yelo.

To the West:

Confessions of a Former Speed Hike Record Attempter-

While on the surface it seemed unrealistic, there was a shot that I could break Jennifer Pharr Davis' unsupported speed record on Vermont's Long Trail. Seven days, fifteen hours and forty minutes to cover 273 miles of difficult to extremely difficult terrain. A hair under 37 miles per day. It's kind of a BS record, mainly noted for the current record holder's subsequent claim to fame as the fastest hiker to traverse the AT. Although she's better known as a pretty swell person too.

Travis Wildeboer holds a faster time, six days, seventeen hours and twenty-five minutes, done self-supported style (without resupply). So without stopping for any supplies he finished it nearly a full day faster than the aforementioned Mrs. Davis. That's why it's a bit of a silly record. BUT...if I could pull it off, I could make the (minor) claim to fame of having bested the queen of the trail. Something no man or woman has yet done. (A very minor technicality lets us not count Travis.) BS or not- this thirty five year old husband, father, and part time hiker thought it would be pretty fun to tell folks about. "I just beat Jennifer Pharr Davis!"

Good headline, you gotta admit it.

But let's be honest, even on the surface it's not that realistic. Although it's been thirteen years since I hiked it, the northern half of the Long Trail is every bit as hard, if not harder, than the vaunted section of the Appalachian Trail through Southern Maine and Northern New Hampshire. The trail could be described as a relatively easy rock climbing trip with an excessive approach trail if you wanted to be kind. If not, you could call it a trail only in the sense that it has blazes to mark the way and some shelters to stay in.

Trail is a misleading word for a pathway with barely a flat spot and interspersed with mud holes, in dry season mind you, up to sixteen inches deep. These are quickly followed by climbs up and down bare rock at angles up to vertical. Technical terms like stemming, smearing, edging, mantel and down-climbing are more accurate ways to describe forward progress than typical terms like walking. Ups and downs? This is a trail that should be the poster child for the term "in between the contour lines." While the map shows a relatively straightforward trail through the mountains, in reality that 50' contour interval on your map only shows the net result of that section travelled. It was not uncommon to find oneself climbing twenty-five feet to descend seventy-five feet. Climbing five feet down, to stand in a mud hole, would quickly be followed by a ten foot climb.

But if this is quickly starting to sound like whining and crying- well I would agree.

It's a tough trail, but not impassible. More importantly, it is heart busting not just for its difficulty; but for its beauty. When you catch your breath and have a chance to taste the air, there is no air finer than the Northwoods as summer draws to a close. The scents are strong, the air is sweet and even the mud has a deep clean earthy smell that's found in few places on the planet. The Northwoods are special any time of year, but as the leaves turn and the full power of autumn takes hold...there are few finer places on earth.

The trail forces you to all fours as you climb and scramble your way along. Forces you to see the amazing world that goes on in these primal woods. Mushrooms, ferns, and ten billion types of mosses form a veritable jungle of miniature forests to explore. Fuzzy caterpillars and other creatures roam this landscape beneath your toes. As you stop to take a breath your eyes take in the rock your hand must grab to haul you up and down the trail. Your hands take in texture, swirls, crystals and other ancient formations. You reach for support from the trees, touching spots worn to a polish by the hands of others that would make any fine furniture maker jealous. Even on the relatively straight sections of trail, your eyes can easily get lost in the wild spider webs of roots that bind the trail to the mountain as you nimbly step upon the toes of trees strong enough to rip apart mountains.

Finally you walk upright in spots, but even these spots are different. Rock and root hopping through some, dancing at the edge of mud holes, balancing on bog bridges both planned and improvised. Traversing sections of bare rock, mossy trail, and evergreen needle blanketed pillows of earth and rocky piles left from nature's demolition squad. You play games of twister with fallen trees and even the winding trail itself with its sudden turns and twists. As you descend you walk streambeds, both active and dry, as water begins to accumulate into small falls, pools, and streams. As you ascend you climb vertical walls, traverse ledges, penetrate mountain peaks and finally stand on the top of the world: the entire beauty, vastness, and limitless wood of the land laid before your eyes.

It's a fine place for a stroll.

Beauty is before me.
Beauty is behind me.
Beauty is below me.
Beauty is above me.
I walk in beauty.

Navajo prayer

The Record Attempt:

I'm losing my love of adventure
I'm losing all respect for me and myself tonight
I wonder what happens if I get to the end of this tunnel
and there isn't a light

I've worn down the treads on all of my tires
I've worn through the elbows and the knees of my clothing
and I'm stumbling down the gravel driveway of desire
trying not to wake up my sleepy self-loathing...

Day zero started off at 1:00 pm, a start time stolen right from the playbook of one Matthew D. Kirk. This unusual start time set me up for a potential overnighter or two, the only real chance I had of popping a record setting time. The plan was to hold around thirty miles a day for the first, and horrendously difficult, 160 or so miles of trail north of The Inn at the Long Trail. After a shower, resupply, good night's rest and a few pints poured by Owen I would make a desperate push over the last 104 miles of the medium to difficult terrain on the southern half of the trail, including the aforementioned all night run to the finish.

Not a realistic plan per say; but the only plan available. While I made a nice push this last year in terms of physical fitness during an extended layoff, I had been back to work for nearly six weeks. What was supposed to be part time employment leading up to this hike quickly turned into fifty hour weeks. What was once a 100-200 mile per week training schedule devolved into two 75 mile in 36 hour long trips interspersed with ten miles or so of jogging. I had my employer's blessing to go for one last hurrah, but nothing more than a two week blitz including travel.

So could a thirty-five year old husband, father, and fairly fast part time fellow run with the elites? I had good gear, good country to travel, and thirty years of experience to back me up. I could hit forty and fifty mile days; and I can pull all-nighters and repeated nights with only four hours of sleep when I needed to. I was hoping to be the anti-record breaker. The regular guy who could combine smarts, experience and sleep deprivation but not all those fancy athletics found among the younger folks pulling these kind of things off. Didn't look good really: but I owed it to myself to try.

I arrived at the Canadian Border around noon after hiking up from the trailhead. I took some time to take in the view, offer a little something to the fella that owns the trail, and pray for speed, safety, and above all, wisdom. This trail is a risky one to begin with; pushing my limits on short rest, hiking in the dark, and negotiating the tricky tread-way called for a little extra ordinary assistance from the powers that be. So I took some time to pay my respects, kissed the boundary marker farewell and headed off at 1:00 pm.

Things didn't go to bad that first day really. It was good to be walking these woods again after twelve years. It was good to be moving at twice the speed I could go in my twenties with gear I made with my own hands. With a pack that weighed half, and a brain at least twice as full of knowledge. It was beautiful. I caught a fellow hiker around dinner time on the summit of Jay Peak; he had shuttled up from Montpelier with me and we had dropped him off to start his hike the previous day. I'd travelled in a handful of hours what he had travelled in a day and a half. I would travel nearly double that still after he stopped to settle in for the night. While I can't say it's anything special one way or the other...well there is something to be said for moving two or three times the speed of your fellow hikers. It's not an arrogance or smug satisfaction, but a deep sense of freedom few will understand.

Night hiking on the north end of the Long Trail is an adventure. Can't say much for safety, intelligence, common sense, avoiding bodily harm or maintaining your sanity; but I can say it's an adventure. At night you don't get cute. No tiptoeing around the mud pits, too risky; straight on through is the only sure footing. No rock hoping down or up an incline, too dangerous; all fours or on your ass is the only option. No good chance of staying on the trail, too hard; but within the first mile or so I learned to feel when I was off trail. The scant leaf cover would get softer, a bit more undergrowth would brush your shins, and believe it or not: you just plain old know you're off trail.

There was a full moon that first night, purely by accident on my part, purely unhelpful. It was plenty bright, but the trail is too tree covered to see by moonlight. It was bright enough to make your night vision suffer and to render ultralight headlamps a wee bit less effective. I learned another fun fact about my good friend the paper birch; it has a slight iridescence by moonlight. While quite pretty on the one hand that fine tree that provides welcome aid to any fire builder traipsing through the Northwoods also provides false blazes to follow by night, making navigation a bit more difficult and distracting. But truthfully I had no complaints; while I can't recommend night hiking as a highly suggested way to spend your time- it's an experience not to be missed at some point in your hiking career.

There was something else I came to learn during this night and my subsequent nocturnal travels; my trail toes were damn good. We speedy folks all like to think we don't stare at our feet in tricky terrain, in fact I may have said as much a few times myself in public places, but the fact of the matter was; when it came time to find the proverbial proof in the pudding, well, my pudding set up quite nicely. I had a chest mounted headlamp, aimed about seven feet or so in front of me, and a mildly dim spot light on my head to search for blazes and find the twists and turns in the route. In short I couldn't look at my toes if I wanted to. And that was fine.

Awhile back a brief discussion on the topic was held at WhiteBlaze, a few theories were laid out, and in my case at least: one was proven. Your eye and brain scan the trail ahead, perhaps memorizing the upcoming obstacles, or perhaps not, and your trail toes figure the rest out. Like a blind man reading brail they find their way smoothly and safely without your direct intervention if you let them. Can't say the wild tread-way was a poor test. Can't say I unconsciously looked at something I couldn't see. You can say, eventually, your feet can take care of themselves if you let them and I was damn proud of my tootsies.

I gave it up for the evening around 1:00 am near a small stream. The stealth camping part of the hike would commence. I took the time to wash up, eat another meal, wash my socks, hang my food, and set up a small stealth camp. Although I eat breakfast in camp, I disappear my camp in the morning and since I'm up early, well I never camped at all as far as anyone is concerned really, and that's what stealth camping means. I was off again by 6:30 or so and because it is confussing to say the least, despite getting some sleep I feel it's fair to warn you I was still in the midst of my first day when I left due to my late afternoon start. Day 1 would officially end at 1:00 pm that afternoon, a very confussing bit of mathematics for a reader, let alone a sleepy hiker, to keep track of.

Day 2 started off pleasant enough after a streamside lunch, but quickly fell apart. My mind fell into unpleasant places, a bad plan on a record attempt. Mainly the unpleasantness had to do with said attempt. After the pleasantness of my long awaited reunion with the Northwoods had faded, I began to realize what I was doing, and why. Or rather; why? This would mark my first record attempt, not speed hike, there had been plenty of those, but record attempt. It seemed that the second that tag was added to the agenda for the hike everything changed.

I couldn't see why, but it clearly had. A choice to pick up the pace, lengthen a stride, or push over a hill was no longer a gentle nudge to see where these legs could take me. Instead it was a mandated action dictated by the attempt. It is pleasant to push a bit, lovely to move as freely and swiftly as any other creature of the forest.

All these normal actions became quite unpleasant, though, once they became not a choice, but a necessity. I don't often take long breaks, but somehow my breaks became impossibly short under the microscope of the attempt. In reality they didn't really change at all, but they felt different. Instead of "let's get back to it!" It became, "you have to get moving again to stay on pace". Looking back I see that there really were no changes, the issues were all mental perception, but it was a perception I was not prepared for.

Every choice, every step, every mile was dictated by the goal. While some folks can do it, or more accurately get over it, I could not. I couldn't reconcile how two words could completely reshape my experience on the trail. I no longer skipped like a deer, danced to the music, flowed through the woods. For the first time in a long time, I fought with the trail. I fought with myself. All over two simple words.

As I lumbered up to a shelter for dinner, the trail provided a solution, or rather it provided a little clarity. This shelter was occupied by two fellas, and not just fellas, but two folks I needed to talk to. Ron Strickland is a published author, lifetime hiker, and founder of the Pacific Northwest Trail. His friend Bart Smith, a photographer for none other than Earl Shaffer among others, was the other occupant. These are the types of folks one hikes to meet. These are the types of folks we would call celebrities if our sport was big enough for such things. These are the types of folks I would normally quickly gather up some wood and convince to spend a pleasant evening (for me) of being vigorously questioned about their lives under the tongue-loosening spell of a campfire.

But today was a day filled with junk, and today these folks got demoted to trash collectors. I knew why I was there. I had tried again to write a book this past year, but I stopped myself about halfway through the backpacking section. I was missing something. There was a hole in my resume, no XX,000 miles of trails hiked, nothing special really. While doing something, and doing it well, for thirty years ought to be enough to leave one feeling qualified to write a book something stopped me. Even if said book was completed, who's buying? I'm nobody. Wife and kids meant that suddenly knocking out a checklist of trails was out of the question but maybe a speed record would get my foot in the door.

Ron and I have a similar mission. Protect what we love. Not by building a trail or maintaining it, although Ron has that covered too, but by sharing the experiences we have on the trail. By getting folks interested. By getting folks out with our writing. Him with tales and history, me with humor, knowledge, and help. Ultimately we strive to protect what we love with the simplest solution of all, get you to fall in love with what we love; then you'll protect it too. We discussed several of the obstacles, many of the dangers facing the land we love and the struggles involved in reaching deep into the hearts and minds of folks.

"You need a stunt." said Bart, perfectly summing it up for me. Publishing was hard enough, but ultimately, it was harder to sell. That's what had stopped me, and these fella's knew that story well. I can't say that they have the answer, but they at least knew the question. They knew the junk in my head, they were walking the path I wanted to walk. Ron's trail name is Pathfinder and I was trying to find mine. If you want to talk trail magic bordering on impossible coincidence, it doesn't get much cleaner than that.

I can't say I made a pleasant companion, can't say I even had anything intelligent to say. I'm actually a bit embarrassed when I look back. I can certainly say I seemed to listen little, but I can say that I understood a lot. Once again that pesky record attempt got in the way of what should have been a fascinating evening spent with two remarkable travelers. It wasn't much, but it was enough. And while I'm sure these two folks counted the evening as nothing more than an encounter with another hiker; it was precious time well spent for me. Trail magic in every sense of the word. And in the typical way such things work- I was deeply affected.

Can't say all was better with the world upon my departure, but it was getting a bit clearer. As I walked off into the dark Bart snapped a few photos and away I went. For a brief time I wasn't on a record attempt, I was just a hiker thinking deep thoughts in the place made for deep thoughts. Just pondering the problems of life as step after step solutions were given. Hiking solves problems, plain and simple. Just like the trail, it doesn't happen all at once. There are some long hard slogs and climbs, occasional vistas of insight, some filler, distraction and fresh encounters to change your perspective. But if you follow the trail till the end, you're rarely disappointed.

The miles melted away, the thoughts died down and dead ended. The day was long ended (per the calendar at least) and it was time for sleep. A dry camp this time, I nonetheless found some dried leaves to clean up the mud spatter from my legs, had a simple dry meal, and made a simple camp. Once again the critical hour of 1:00 arrived and I turned in for the evening. 5:30 came quickly, 6:30 came a bit quicker, not the quickest of starts, but overall a fast enough turn around to enter the home stretch of record attempt day two, and the beginning of calendar day three. Record attempt day three would begin at 1:00 pm. If nothing else, this inappropriate way to count time should be enough of a warning that things get silly when the dreaded words are added to the trip.

Native Americans have a general belief that the winged ones (birds) are the messengers of the Great Spirit. While every tribe has a different view of such things, and some birds have specific medicine, all birds are generally regarded as close to the creator. Finding a feather, for lack of any other specific meaning attached to the bird it came from, was generally seen as a message. A pretty simple one; generally "Hello".

I find feathers often when I hike, and you may see me on the trail with a bit of a collection accumulating in my long hair. I get a bit of a boost when I get a passing nod from the fella that owns the place. On this hike though there were no feathers to be found, a bit of a bad sign really. But as day two drew to a close I found one; a single turkey feather about 14" long laid out kindly on the trail for me to find. Now while some omens and portents may require the assistance of a medicine man or council of elders to sort out, this one was pretty straight forward; "Be thankful." So I stuck it in my hair as usual, one lone feather. One message I wouldn't learn the meaning of until later in the trip.

Later that day I ran into a hiker who stopped me to take my picture. Be-feathered and wearing my sexy skirt I apparently made a fantastic photo opportunity. Turns out it was a fella I knew from

WhiteBlaze, named Florida Mike and I introduced myself. "You're Just Bill! You're doing that speed hike thing right?" We chatted a bit, he mentioned he didn't just get a good laugh, which is never to be underrated, but that he got a few tidbits of good advice from me every once in a while too. While that record attempt thing didn't seem to be going too great at the moment, the helping folks out thing was proving to be going well. I would run into other folks along the way, many of them living in the outskirts of the online trail community in the fine town known as Lurkerville. Many of them didn't care to admit that they spent any time on WhiteBlaze, but they all knew me when asked, and most had some nice things to say.

Not long after I hit a shelter where some hikers were following the sage advice of one Paul "Mags" Magnanti. A former Long Trail thru-hiker and his lady-friend were out for a quick overnighter. They'd hiked in about four miles from the trailhead and thankfully followed Mags most solemn and critical advice, "Less Gear, More Beer!" Leading them to offer said beer to this thirsty traveler. I hate IPAs. I hate warm beer. The smiling hiker handed me a warm IPA as he sat down to chat. It was a fantastic beer.

Things were starting to look up. I knew a record was slipping away, but some of the worst of the edge had been taken off. I can't say I was happy, but I no longer completely hated my guts. The previous night's companions, some ego boosting encounters with the online community in the real world, pleasant weather, unbelievable woods- and a beer. Record attempt or not, things were decent.

Which is why things turned so shockingly fast on me. I know the point it all went wrong really. It was by far the lowest moment I've ever reached while on trail. I have done some severely questionable things in my time as a hiker. In my youth I even reached the scumbag trifecta: hiker/climber/paddler. Simply hiking in and of itself generally leaves you on shaky ground with town folks to begin with. And even by hiker standards I've been known to dirt bag it on several occasions, even to sink so low as to clearly enter the subculture of hiker trash. Hikers are often seen as fairly low on the social spectrum, I have occasionally seen the bottom of the bottom on even that scale of low moral standards. But that day: I finally crossed a line.

As I reached the top of Whiteface Mountain I stopped to take the obligatory photo. One of the problems with setting a record is that the burden of proving that you have set said record lies on you. Your personal honor and reputation, coupled with a resume of past accomplishments are the main qualifiers. For a no name like me, extensive photos of every notable intersection, signpost, landmark, and anything else you can get your hands on are important. Sitting at home going through my photos I flip through stupid picture after stupid picture of signs, and me standing next to signs. So once more I snapped pictures of myself, not in breathtaking Vermont, but of me standing in front of a brown sign.

With that disgust and self-loathing in mind I next did the unforgivable. I looked at that sign. It told me that a mere twenty or thirty steps to my left lay the true summit of Whiteface, and more importantly a likely scenic overlook at said summit. I could see the opening through the trees. The sign also indicated that to my right, the Long Trail continued south. The summit was not on the trail. I had spent several hours reaching this lackluster sign and non-view twenty paces from the peak. It was mid-afternoon, bright, clear, barely a cloud in the sky. This was Vermont in late September, in all its leaf changing autumn glory. In fact, I am quite sure those few thin wispy clouds that were around would only have enhanced the view. But I wouldn't know.

I went right.

I reached Sterling Pond Shelter around six or so. It should have been dinner time, but I wasn't interested. The shelter was crowded, once more with good folks that I wouldn't be visiting with really. I sat down and changed socks and let my feet air out. I talked with a super cute hiker from Asheville. Told me all about how that bitch Jennifer Pharr Davis was a super southern sweetie and would be a great person even if she never hiked more than a fifteen mile day. She saw my taped up foot and we talked blisters. I hooked her up with some Leukotape (always the helpful fellow) as she could find no tape to help her with her frequent blisters. The record attempt demanded that 600-800 calories be ingested at this time, but the record attempt would have to be happy with the fact that instead of hanging out with a shelter full of neat folks to talk to, I would be pushing on into the cold wind that had been building for the last few hours.

I told them I was on a record attempt. I told them I had to keep hiking. It was literally incomprehensible to them. It was about dark, it was cold, and it was not time to hike. We were at a shelter. I was actually leaving? Yes. Why? Because I'm stupid. Finally as it became quite clear to all the disbelieving folks at the shelter (including myself) that I actually was leaving they wished me luck. One of the weekenders drove the nail in the coffin as I walked away, "Remember, this is supposed to be fun!"

It's not.

As I headed over the summit of Spruce Peak the fog rolled in ahead of the brisk cold air. In short order I found myself in a fog induced white out. To make matters worse, I had taken a bad fall in the dip between the two peaks. My downhill foot slid away from me on the fog dampened rock, leaving my toe pinned on the rock edge I had been using for a foothold. As I fell my toe snagged in a severely enforced quadriceps stretch. As the flames exploded in my quad I instinctively rolled hard to my left, slamming my hip into the rock but freeing my toe as I rolled the last few feet down the eight foot drop. I rolled for a bit as I tried to straighten my left leg. I could have sworn I tore my quad. I bruised my hip fairly badly in the process, but I managed to get to my feet and start shambling along. It would take a few hours to walk it out, but my quad proved to be intact. I would be painfully reminded each night for the next week not to roll onto my left hip at night.

It would take about eight more hours to figure out that I had broken my left pinkie toe in the fall. But at the moment there were bigger concerns. Visibility was down to about 10 feet, about five with my headlamp on as full darkness settled in. I found the warming hut at the top of Spruce Peak, but despite being told it was open, it was not. I should have stopped. But it was too early. I was too high up for the weather. I was on a record attempt. Injuries, bad weather, pain; part of the deal. You know the drill; keep moving.

I would ultimately become lost in that whiteout. Not really lost, but backpacker lost. I knew more or less where I was, I just wasn't on the trail. There was a recent relocation there, but I'm sure it makes perfect sense in the daytime. The trail looped around the peak then headed down, my compass told me I was on that trail, and the wind changing direction on my face reported the same. Somewhere I missed the turn off, if there was one. I passed the Elephant's Foot Trailhead, with its blue blazed tree and sign. That may have been it. Either way, I eventually ended up walking about 3-5 miles out of my way down Spruce Peak and into the Stowe Mountain Resort. I road walked back to the trail and walked a few hundred feet up the trail and went to bed on the foot of Mt. Mansfield.

Unless I doubled back, the record attempt was over, you don't get a record for not hiking on a trail. (I still had vague hopes.) To add insult to injury, I failed to pay attention to my camp. Everyone said rain on Sunday (tomorrow afternoon). But the earth said rain tonight. The wind shift, the temperature drop, the fog; all of it screamed that the rain was early. None of the screaming reached my brain.

Too stubborn to listen to the land I laid down right on the trail. I didn't even pitch my tent, just laid in it. And that would be all I would do. It poured. I set up on the trail, at the bottom of a 4000' tall mountain, at the bottom of a five mile long waterfall. At times an inch of rain flowed through my shelter. It was cold. Since it was a record attempt, I packed my lightest bag, an 11.25 ounce homemade synthetic quilt. While my massive ego forces me to mention that the quilt did its job, and I didn't die, that's really all I can say. Low 40's, likely dropped into high 30's, soaking wet, worn out from the hike, injury, and not eating. Well that's the kind of thing you read about in the obituary notices.

I had been warned. Spiritually, emotionally, mentally, the trail that often speaks so kindly and clearly to me told me this record attempt thing wasn't kosher. The warnings were subtle, then not so subtle, then blatantly obvious. When all those failed it became painfully obvious. I was physically warned, slapped down and busted up. If I wouldn't stop, the trail would stop me.

As the throbbing in my foot began to diagnose itself I lay there in my state of not sleeping but not dying. The trail had had enough. I had had enough. To make sure though, it rained until dawn. Just to make sure I got the message, it stayed wet and cold enough to prevent sleep. Just to be absolutely positively certain I had learned the error of my ways, I laid in the dark until I shivered the lesson all the way to the core of the disappointing sorry ass hiker I had become.

...It takes a stiff upper lip
just to hold up my face
I gotta suck it up and savor the taste of my own behavior
I am spinning with longing
faster than a roulette wheel
this is not who I meant to be,
this is not how I meant to feel

Ani DiFranco, "Wish I may"

The Interlude at The Inn:

Every single night, I endure the flight
Of little wings of white-flamed
Butterflies in my brain
These ideas of mine
Percolate the mind
Trickle down the spine
Swarm the belly, swelling to a blaze

That's when the pain comes in
Like a second skeleton
Trying to fit beneath the skin
I can't fit the feelings in, oh
Every single night's a light with my brain...

Well come the next morning I did what any sane, non-record attempting hiker would do, I went to the Stowe Mountain Resort and had the all you can eat breakfast buffet. Not that great considering the $275 dollar a night hiker rate at said resort, but the manager was kind and happy to help a broken and soaked hiker out by firing up the fake fireplace and letting me spread some gear on the $500 a piece leather chairs sitting around the bar.

After a bit of debate over made to order omelets and what I assume to be Quebec'er style boiled ham and flavorless sausage. I packed up and hitched to Stowe, then to Duxbury. I hobbled across Waterbury to a better location and hitched down to Waitsfield, then a few miles more to Irasville. This looked like the end of the hitchhiking road and my throbbing foot. So I found a local cab company and got a ride the last stretch to The Inn at Long Trail.

Owen was relegated to pouring a consolation pint or three and serving a paddy melt in lieu of the planned refuel on the way to Jennifer Pharr Davis ass kicking glory I had originally planned. I caught the Bears game, had some pleasant conversations with the runners staying there who had just participated in the Spartan Run.

All in all not a bad evening for a busted attempt, but though I saw them at the end of the bar that night, I couldn't bring myself to talk to the hikers I saw. I BS'd a bit with Owen, rocked out my skirt for the runners who appreciate a nice set of legs, and nodded off on the couch sometime in the third quarter of the game.

The following morning I began to come up with some kind of plan, but first it was time for breakfast, time to face my fellow hikers. An elderly woman joined us because she just loved to hear us hikers talk. A fine lass about my age was in company, who was just back on trail after taking two weeks off for a foot infection. She'd apparently learned who I was from WhiteBlaze while she was laid up, so we chatted a bit, but I do apologize because I was a bit overbearing in the conversation at our table that morning as I had some business to attend to.

Also in attendance were a couple of Southbound AT hikers from my neck of the woods, the fella lived a half hour away, and the spunky lass forty-five minutes or so. They were moving SLOW, but despite his occasional laments on that regard, she was filled with smiles and laughs every time he told me about finding her neck deep in berry patches or soaking her feet in a stream. They were having a fantastic time, but there was a problem there somewhere so I dug it out.

Eventually the table cleared and the three of us were left alone and he broached the embarrassing subject of trouble. The chafe monster had been plaguing him for the last three months or so since leaving Katahdin. In addition they were out of stove fuel and facing the prospect of a long delay as they went to the next town to get some before they could head out. Now some folks think trail magic works a certain way, but I can tell you it doesn't always go the way you think. Lest you think too highly of me, these folks were put here for me, and not I for them. I had some bad medicine from my attempt to make up for: nothing more than that.

So I diagnosed his issue, provided some sage advice on the subjects of crotch rot, friction and salt buildup. Interestingly in his case, the low mile days were making it worse, he was hiking just enough to develop a problem, but not enough for it to get really bad, which would have built a tough patch up after it healed. Now at that point I would have given the shirt off my back to make things right with the trail, but that wouldn't help him much. So I did the next best thing; I gave him the skirt off my ass.

As some of you may know I will note with heavy sarcasm the sheer improbable coincidence that happens during such encounters. It just so happened that I had a resupply box at the inn. And it just so happened that I chose to use, for the first time in two years, an isobutane canister stove for this trip, and that a spare was in the resupply box. It also happens that I was trying out coconut oil, for just such a hiker related condition on this trip, for the first time in my life mind you, and a few ounces of it was in said box. It also just so happens that I had just started making skirts for hikers, to solve this very problem for myself. It just so happened that I broke my toe, left the trail, caught just the right hitches and local services to arrive at this inn which sits at the junction of the AT and Long Trail at the exact same time as this troubled couple who live a short drive from my house halfway across the country as we both travelled through the trails of Vermont.

As mentioned, clearly simple happenstance.

So I headed up to retrieve them from my room; skirt, fuel, and soothing balm in hand I sent the fella back on the trail. He was quite ecstatic, amazed, and a bit bewildered by his seeming good fortune. But as I said, the trail magic in this case came in the form of an unsettled debt owed by yours truly to the trail and he was merely an unwilling bystander in the whole affair.

I'm not always a nice guy, but I always pay what I owe, and my tab was run up pretty high.

So for those of you who've never experienced it:

That's how trail magic works from the other side of the exchange.

...That what I am is what I am cause I does what I does
And maybe I'd relax, let my breast just bust open
My heart's made of parts of all that surround me
And that's why the devil just can't get around me

Every single night's a light, every single night's a fight
And every single fight's alright with my brain...

I just wanna feel everything
I just wanna feel everything
I just wanna feel everything
I just wanna feel everything"

Fiona Apple, "Every single night"

The Speed Hike:

Once in a great while all the aspects of walking come together, and then I have an hour or a day when I simply glide along, seemingly expending no energy. When this happens, distance melts under my feet, and I feel as though I could stride on forever. I can't force such moments and I don't know where they come from, but the more I walk, the more often they happen. Not surprisingly, they occur most often on really long treks. On these days, I've walked for five hours and twelve miles and more without a break, yet with such little effort that I don't realize how long and how far I've traveled until I finally stop. I never feel any effects afterward either, except perhaps, a greater feeling of well-being and contentment.

Chris Townsend, "The Backpackers's Handbook"

So debts settled and a little time left before I had to rush back to the grind. I put the second part of my plan into effect. I'd not come south for no reason, the Long Trail and the AT overlap for the last hundred miles or so, and while I was in no shape for a record breaker across the north half of the trail, I figured worst case I could do a little hobbling around on the easier southern section. I still wasn't sure how or where, but things tend to work out.

Vermont's excellent local bus system picked me up and I headed to Rutland, two dollars exact change only. In Rutland I had a fine lunch at Griffin House, where the owner informed me that he lived two blocks from my current home for several years before returning to his native Vermont. We discussed how last time I was here the state was divided. How the rural homes I had passed all displayed their "Take Vermont Back" signs in their yard. How a silly thing like who wants to marry whom had ripped apart the place. And how a not so silly thing as Mother Nature's helper Irene had brought it back together. "I am Vermont Strong" license plates now replaced the signs and a fine state was made whole again.

Two dollars exact change brought me to Manchester Center. Where another bus would have carried me to Bennington, but alas there was only a dollar left from the five I had broken at the Inn. My bus ride was over. While the bulk of the Long Trail map has very little information on side trails, the Lye Brook Trail at the edge of town was conveniently listed, and I headed over to check it out.

Busted foot, no stove fuel, six days of left over 5500 calorie two and a half pound per day record attempting food stuffed into my pack I headed across town and up the trail. Where for the first time in over a year of this speed hike kick, I stopped before dark.

Long practiced hands quickly prepared my stealth camp. A fire sprang from damp wood and quickly settled into coals for making dinner. Old skills rarely practiced in a record setting pace came back smoothly and easily. As I gently coaxed my small fire it warmed my bare legs and lightly dressed "camp clothes are for camping not speed hiking" body as the temps settled into the forties. I warmed a pot of tea, laid a few inches from my Indian style fire and took in the stars. It went quickly and efficiently, not because I was in a hurry, but because this is what I know how to do.

I slept till I felt like it. Ate breakfast, lingered over coffee, and restored my camp back to the state it bore when I arrived. I even read a little, using my Jobs-a-ma Phone for something other than taking pictures of signs was a welcome break. I made it up to the breathtaking Stratton Pond, took a divine stroll around its southern edge, and had a lazy lunch over the trail journal at the shelter. I skipped Stratton, saving my foot the worst of it, taking the side trails instead to see new trail and make it to the next shelter to see if there were some folks to visit with.

I suppose I've been calling it speed hiking because that's what other folks call it. Really it has little to do with your speed, or your miles. Sure there's a bit of physical and philosophical work involved. You have to be in some type of shape, and round doesn't count. You have to pare down your gear, not just for weight, but for simplicity. Your mind needs to shift a bit, you need to put the pieces together until the hiking is just motion. Until it's easy. The pack doesn't drag on you, you cut it down to just the necessities.

The gear doesn't complicate things, it complements the few tasks you've left to yourself as you perfect your style. The walking is just what you do, same as breathing.

My new friend Ron enjoys learning the history of things, oral tradition and the folks who've lived and travelled the lands we cross. I have the same fascination with the folks who didn't visit, or recreate, or get away from anything. I have always admired the people who lived with the land, who lived the lesson that many backpackers come to learn; we live not in towns or houses, but on the planet earth. The natives of this land we travel were always home, and so was I.

While it's unfair to generalize the beliefs of Native Americans, there is a concept they mostly all agree with. Not all members of this race believed there was a fella that owned the place and even those that do were honest enough to admit they didn't have all the answers. The word for God is most often said to translate to "Great Spirit", but more accurately translates to "Great Mystery" an endearing bit of humble honesty I always enjoy.

But they do all agree that there is something generally called the Spirit That Moves Through All Things. A power that connects us all, and by us, they mean everyone and everything. The same things the folks at the edges of multiple disciplines of science continue to discover. It is the medicine behind trail magic, the connection our greatest minds explore in concepts like quantum mechanics and string theory. Seems most of the time you look hard, it's the thing behind nearly any native people, any spiritual practice, any walk in the woods.

The medicine wheel has its seven directions; east, west, south, north, above, and below. The seventh for you astute counters, is two directions at once. This direction represents the Great Mystery, as well as the center. It represents the infinite and a very finite spot all in one. It is the location where an individual's connection to the Spirit That Moves Though All Things is located. From this location, from this one small speck of the vast life in the universe; all things are connected.

It is in this location that I speed hike.

I checked the time and the map, I was back on the AT after my short cut and short forest service road walk on the way to Kid Gore Shelter. While I couldn't tell you exactly, I'd travelled a bit over four miles. In just a hair over an hour. Not too shabby, even without a broken foot or ten pounds of extra food, in fact, that's about as fast as a hiker can move without running.

People ask what I think about when I hike, and that's often too complicated to answer. But the last few paragraphs are the thoughts I had during that four mile stretch. You see I do think when I hike. I think completely. When I speed hike I do so in the center, or I can't do it at all. My body does its thing, I am not unaware of it, but just like you can make a conscious effort to note the fact that you are still breathing, most of the time you do so with little notice or effort on your part. Speed hiking isn't the happy ignorance of the drunk, or the dull distance of the dope smoker. It's not even the distraction of the daydreamer.

It's simply the absence of effort. A connection to the land, to the spirit that moves through it, to the medicine that flows there. When I hike in that state I am fully aware, clearly participating, at full capacity. If not, well I'm just another guy, just a hiker, just walking. Just moving at the speed the trail will let me, just covering two miles an hour or less. Just thinking about things that hikers just think about. Mileage, food, water, camp, food, your pack, the next hill, the next downhill, and food. Sometimes I'm just a hiker. But sometimes I'm the fastest guy on the trail, sometimes I dance, I flow, I travel at speeds I have no business travelling at.

I stayed with some folks at Kid Gore shelter. Section hikers from Illinois, a soldier on leave, a LT hiker about to finish a southbound trip, and a fella who got in long after dark. The thru-hiker was in bed well before dark, the section hikers snuggled in bed by seven. I shared some of my food with the soldier, some good jerky and sausage to supplement his MRE that was consumed faster than I could cut a hunk of jerky. I had a fire, watched the sunset, saw the stars, sat and watched the wind blow in a valley while everyone else went to sleep, so they could push some miles. Nobody shared the fire. None of them smelled the roses. I understood.

The next day I hiked with the late nighter, a sixty one year old from Maine who was section hiking down the trail. We had a pleasant talk as we walked to the fire tower on Glastonbury. Lest you think I was moving quickly the previous day and all better, that my injury was not quite as bad as Ol' Bill made out; for the first time in ten years something quite unusual happened to me. The sixty-one year old section hiker, with his forty pound pack, asked me how far to the fire tower. Because although the conversation was pleasant, well, you see, I was really slowing him down.

We parted ways at the shelter, I was heading to Williamstown via Bennington, and he via the AT. I had a twelve mile hike from the shelter where our trails parted ways. I was thinking my foot wouldn't hold out, and I'd need to take two days to make the remaining miles. It was around 10:00, I made it before 3:00, completely on accident.

I'd horribly paraphrased that quote from Mr. Townsend I used at the beginning of this section earlier in the trip, when his name came up in discussion with Ron and Bart. I told them it was my favorite quote, perhaps from any outdoorsman. Oddly I only read one of his books, not even the one I quoted. One day in the library doing some research I found his book, opened it to a random page and read that quote. Of no relation to Chris, just one of those trail co-winky-dinks, my last name is also Townsend, I'd just walked twelve miles in five hours, I'd just finished my trip with a sense of well-being and contentment.

I slipped into the flow a few times. Stopped to enjoy the views and the white rocks along the way too. I thought about the problems I'd had. I thought about the problem we all have; that if folks don't fall in love with the woods they won't protect them. I thought about how we try to get folks involved, the stories we tell about backpacking. About hardships endured, weather battled, mountains conquered, miles covered. It doesn't actually sound pleasant does it? It's a bit of an exclusive club really, I think most of us know the rewards, I think many of us have had a burst or two of speed hiking themselves. I think most of you get it. Maybe, it's time to start talking about it.

It's not just walking, it's not just backpacking, they aren't just the dirty, bug infested, man-eating bear filled woods that only a select few can enter. The trail won't always be there. It only exists because some folks love it. Just day hikers, just clueless weekenders, just section hikers, just thru-hikers, just speed hikers, just people who care. Just people who walk around.

I pulled the feather from my hair, to secure it for the trip home. I'd asked for wisdom, I'd committed a serious transgression, I'd made up for it , and I'd come out to do what I planned to do. I'd remembered that if I travel right, I'm faster than damn near anyone around. Except I'm not, and it doesn't matter, unless I'm part of the whole. It doesn't come when I want it, or fight for it, or try. It comes when I don't, when I help, when I teach others, when I slow down and drink deep of all the land has to offer, when I remember my place, and when I'm thankful for it.

I'm not a record setter. I came up with the name Just Bill as a bit of a joke, the name I use when I'm just out and about. Not doing anything special, not thru-hiking or breaking a record. Just doing stuff that doesn't require or deserve an official trail name. Just like the Indians who had a common name, but took on a secret name, a medicine name when they wished to tap into the power of the spirit that moves though all things. I believe these days we call them trail names. I believe there's little difference.

So I couldn't pull off a stunt. I won't have anyone beating down my door to write a book. But I can finish it now, I wasn't missing anything. Nothing against the records, the XX,000 miles hiked. I hope I can one day claim some of those things still, if for no other reason than they involve a lot of time spent on the trail. But those will come in time, for now, I can go back to doing what I do best. Just hiking, just writing, just helping, just teaching, just joking, just telling some tales about the things folks don't want to tell tales about.

Sure we can keep saying it's just walking, it's just hard, just suck it up; the truth is that's all part of it. Let the trail sort out who deserves to know the secrets, and keep the secrets to ourselves.

But if we want to save it, if we want to protect it, we're going to have to start talking about the secret parts, about what we love.

About how most of the time I am *just* Bill, and that's just fine. It's hard to explain, hard to teach, hard to inspire others to seek it out, it sounds unbelievable, makes you sound crazy to say it, but sometimes that's just backpacking. And sometimes, it's not. Sometimes trail magic is a little more than it seems, sometimes you can move faster than you're able, sometimes it's a whole lot more than hardship, challenge and reward; sometimes it's as easy and essential as breathing.

Sometimes I walk on the trail, sometimes I walk with it, sometimes I walk right off the edge into the center of the universe.

Not bad for just walking.

Thanks for reading-

Just Bill

I wish: I want to stay here.
I wish: this be enough.
I wish: I only love you.
I wish: simplicity.

Look at the speed out there,
it magnetizes me to it,
and I have no fear.
I'm only in to this to; Enjoy!
Bjork, "Enjoy"

To the North:
Goodnight-

Only the old woodsman turns out sleepily, at two bells in the middle watch, after the manner of hunters, trappers, and sailors, the world over. He quietly rebuilds the fire, reduces a bit of navy plug to its lowest denomination, and takes a solitary smoke- still holding down his favorite log.

Nessmuk-George W. Sears, "Woodcraft and Camping"

Well my friend, it is late. Hiker midnight is long past, as is true midnight and the last lone calls of the owl. By any scale by which you choose to measure it, it is time to turn in. Yar, that last one was a fine way to end it if I do say so myself, and I do. A little longer than some, it wound around a bit, as I'm wont to do from time to time, but we got to the right place eventually I suppose.

A proper end to a fine bit of tale telling and perhaps best left at that. So rather than douse the fire and leave a soggy mess for the next passerby, let's bank it up proper so it may burn down clean and cold. Say good evening an pleasant dreams, tuck in, don't ask the question. In the morning we'll hike again!

Dear reader, new friend, I humbly suggest you read no further. No better ending can be found than the one previously shared in the last tale. This is no cheap literary stunt mind you, but a fair piece of advice as we've reached the final bend in this trail. Get out and enjoy your own walk, the book and I will patiently await your return when you're ready.

Happily ever after is nice, but on the trail it's little more than another signpost. Even if you reach the terminus of a trail; you still have to hike back to the trail head, hitch a ride, make your way back to town, catch a bus, train, or plane. Walk through the front door and flip over the hourglass.

So sit on that final stretch of trail, have a happily ever after for a bit, that's what that last signpost is for. At the end all that remains is to go home.

"Why print it at all then, you lying devil?"

Well you paid your bit of coin, committed your precious time to reading my tales. All stories have an end, all tellers are compelled to write one. Part of the deal, as it were.

Hopefully you take a break, enjoy the tales for a while and let your mind wander. Smell the roses as they say.

Eventually, the end will come up, as it always does, so it's unfair not to share it.

Just remember, it's the journey and all that... The end is just the final marker, a destination. But necessary just the same.

Quietly while you were asleep
The moon and I were talking
I asked that she'd always keep you protected...
Sade Adu, "The Sweetest Gift"

Below:
The End-

"Okay JB... is this a tall tale or is it the TRUTH? I didn't believe you at first when you told us about this "encounter" on a thread a while ago. After questioning you a bit on that thread, I did believe you.

Now, I'm not sure."

Karen "HikerMom" Dillard in conversation with the author on WhiteBlaze.net

So, if you're ready, if you must...

"Ah's me...I thought we might get away clean and neat, but I can see in your eyes we're not quite done are we?" And it's true. It seemed strange how he let it burn down to coals during that last tale. Picking bits of wood and unburned stubs as he spoke. Sorting, sifting and piling them so they were all burned up. Causing brief bursts of tickling flames and light to erupt as the coals faded away. Much like the yarn-spinner before you this bit of work seemed to be more of the same show-off bullshit. Likely it was, you realize, but you can recognize the practical matter of it now as well.

You sit watching Just Bill tend to the final act of the fire. As the warm glow fades and the chill of the night soaks into your bones the warmth of the nearby sleeping bag calls to you. The excitement of the tale has worn off, the cold night shaking off the drowse induced by his sleepy monotone. Now sitting in darkness, the mystical bubble between dark and light has popped, you face the grey outline of your evenings companion. In the somber sobriety of this black and white world your logical mind returns to functioning status.

You can tell he's seen it before; the hesitation, the doubt, even the anger. There is some hope in him you'll just say thanks for the company. *Long nights and pleasant days to you Bill. You sense he's had this conversation before. You don't want to ask it, but some things can't be helped. Some questions inevitable and fundamental within the curious minds of those bold enough to step into the woods.*

Each question is a little different, some notable point in a particular tale perhaps. Or even a more general question on some topic or concept. Some queries lighthearted, some with the intensity that only comes from the depths of your soul. But no matter how you phrase it, or pose it, the question at its core is always the same. So you must ask;

"Just Bill, are you really a liar?"

On hands and knees he leans over the fire, giving a steady blow to the last of the coals and unburnt bits. With dirty fingers he pokes and prods the last few chunks. He gazes up at you. Level even, as they used to say. There is just enough moonlight to see each other's eyes. No bruised ego at the accusation, no emotion. And per the unwritten rules, no hard feelings. He draws in one more deep breath, not for an explanation, but for the fire.

His wind brings a flaring glow to the coals, but no more. A fresh wisp of smoke stoked from the coals trails off lazily as he settles back onto his haunches and watches the dark pit. The smoke trails to the heavens, lit by the moonlight as if some silken strand dropped from a giant spider. Suddenly, the smoke puffs out and a small flame shoots up, like blowing out a candle backwards. A smile flashes on his face, directed at the fire as he admires Iktomi's little trick.

Finally, he turns to you to answer your question. With the last gasp of firelight dancing in his eyes, he gives you an answer,

"Sometimes."

The Truth:

It was a close place. I took it up, and held it in my hand. I was a-trembling, because I'd got to decide, forever, betwixt two things, and I knowed it. I studied a minute, sort of holding my breath, and then says to myself:

"All right, then, I'll go to hell" - and tore it up.

Mark Twain, "The Adventures of Huckleberry Finn"

And with that profound statement, a fictional boy, in a fictional book, written by a fictional author stated a truth that Samuel Langhome Clemens himself was incapable of saying in his own words. A work of fiction need not be a lie, and some things are best told in the form of one. Now I'm no Twain, no Clemens either, though I did spin you a yarn or two you hopefully enjoyed.

The Native Americans tell of a language that all speak, the Language of the Heart. Through medicine stories of various sorts passed from one generation to the next, in the feelings one gets when confronted with the powers of the world, and in the soul of all beings that exist, this language is universally understood.

Although the truth is, it takes some effort. There have been a few tales, a few characters involved, and it's more than fair to say I haven't quoted them word for word, nor occasionally struggled to translate this language into a written form.

Maybe I have failed in that job from time to time, and a bit of healthy skepticism on the matter is quite understandable. I hold no grudge. So if you've found yourself doubting the authenticity and the lies told, try to translate the words back to the Language of the Heart from which they originate.

Factual fellas, talking animals, misremembered trips, dubious events, or fictitious conversations aside, if the words ring true in your heart and the ideas sit rightly in your soul when they land there, worry not from whence they came.

The reality:

"The only thing I had control over was myself and my attitude. When I finally realized that, that was the moment the trail started to get easy."

Jennifer Pharr Davis, Badass

We live in cities, towns, and structures we call home. Me too, hell I even build them. We are a generally comfortable people insulated from the outdoors. Occasionally we set out into this hostile place and do battle with the forces of nature. Pitting our wits against the land and braving the wilderness. Occasionally it's shockingly beautiful, peaceful, serene. More often it's dirty, smelly, tough, raining, too hot, too cold, rough, inhospitable; an alien world.

So despite me cherry picking a few overly romantic highlights and notions to share, it's taken a fair bit of time to accumulate them, my whole life in point of fact. It hasn't all been sunshine, yoga instructors, talking coyotes and rainbows. There were many empty miles, chilly rains, injuries, hardships, and defeats. The reality is, it's a fight for town folk to enter the woods.

But this fight has a certain appeal; so you lace up your gloves, enter the ring, and spar with the Ol' fearsome Bitch Ma Nature. At first you're slapped silly and can't stay on your feet. Or worse, she sneers in indifference and you leave the ring in shame. Eventually you learn a few tells, the shrug that precedes her lightning jab, a toe wiggle that warns you to step lightly. You bob, weave, dodge. You learn to hold your own for a bit more each bout. She'll still knock your teeth in if you don't watch it, but you've learned to make it ten rounds. Eventually you may try to land a blow of your own. It's easily absorbed or avoided by the Ancient Lady, but it does draw a smile.

With few exceptions, the natural world contains few doting parents. It can be a sink or swim, fly or die, kill or be killed sorta place for its many full time residents. It wastes little time on those who don't belong, or can't hold their own. It can be a devastatingly uncaring place.

Though a stern parent, your Mother has done you right. You'll get comfy in the ring, make it through the bout, and begin to enjoy the reward in the effort. In short, you'll find you belong.

The reality is that we don't live in towns, cities, or houses; we live on the planet earth. No matter how many walls you put up, fine shingles over your head, nor how deeply you detach in hiding from the world around you, you live here. Your temporary residence simply a little world of your own sitting on the surface of the real world outside your door. On the day you see that, you'll smile at your sparring partner, drop your guard and quit the fight. If all went well, you're all grown up fine and strong; and your Mother will give you a big hug.

Though don't be too shocked if she smacks you upside the head from time to time if you mess up or get careless, even the kindest of mothers do that often enough no matter how old or wise their children become.

Reality is a double edged sword.

The facts:

"No word of a lie."

The Trail Show

Clever words and mystical mumbo jumbo. Bullshit, lies, stories and another white man making a cheap steal from the red man. A laugh or two and some sappy romance easy enough to get caught up in I suppose. Likely a decent enough and well-meaning fella who knows his way around the ol' keyboard fair enough, but the fact is who knows the truth? And if you can't separate the fact from the fiction then what's the point; it's all garbage.

And the fact is you ain't far from wrong. Whether every word is a lie, every explanation a clever excuse, or the words of a crazy man matters little. Whether Just Bill is a figment of my mind or some well-traveled adventurer is not that important.

Many things are plausible enough, some things certainly less so, sometimes we may have the facts and the fiction mixed up despite our best efforts. But it matters little; truthfully and truly, cross my heart and hope to lie.

Who can say what pot Coyote shits in. So whither you blazed from cover to cover like some speed hiking end to ender and missed all the roses. Or day hiked a chapter at a time as you plopped your poops on your porcelain throne ruminating in your own perfume; I'm the only one that knows the facts.

And I'm a lying son of a Bitch.

There is one fact that is certain and we can all agree on. No matter what did or didn't happen. If it happened at all, it happened to me. And as you are not me, it might as well not have happened at all. Who cares really one way or the other. Because it didn't happen to you.

In point of fact, all you did is read a book.

Nothing more, nothing less. You kindly paid me some coin to hear my lies, and I thank ya' truly. I may or may not use the money to take a trip. So now that you're all paid up, the truth is free.

The truth is the Earth is located conveniently in the everywhere just outside your door. The reality is that nothing at all may happen to you. The fact is, only you can find out for certain.

People often demand the facts. You're a people. Go out and get them.

When you get back, I may even believe the stories you tell, but probably not, most people don't.

Worse case; at least you'll be lying on the trail.

Glossary-

General stuff and made-up words:

Confussing-
When something is said, done or thought about that is so confusing, bewildering, or just plain stupid enough to cause injury to the brain resulting in concussion like symptoms.

Reversal of Fortune-
The Ol' Man's slang for puking your guts out.

Jeremiah Johnson-
A popular film featuring a trapper/mountain man played by Robert Redford. The main character leaves town behind.

Keith Shaw-
Former owner of "Shaw's", a popular hiker hostel in Monson, ME. He has departed this world at age 75 in 2004 to seek better competition at the great horseshoe pit in the sky.

Sai- A form of address meaning sir or madam.

Big K- Short for Katahdin.

Baxter-
Refers to Baxter State Park, within whose boundaries Katahdin rests if you refer to a map. Katahdin itself seems not to care.

Trig-
A real word, in this book though it serves as slang for clever.

Jobs-a-ma-phone-
A fairly clever and non-trademark infringing name for a very popular cellular device created by the late Steve Jobs. The phone contains an assistant with a name that sounds Japanese to me. I asked her, but you know how that works out.

Northwoods-
A general term for the types of forests (ecosystems) found from Minnesota to Maine and north into Canada.

Esbit Tabs-
A brand of solid fuel used in backpacking stoves. Military folks may be familiar with Hexamine, a chemical tab used in the same way.

AT (Appalachian Trail)-
Runs 2200 miles from Springer Mountain, Georgia to Katahdin in Maine. It's quite a trail.

LT (Long Trail)-
Runs 273 miles up Vermont from border to border. It's a hell of a trail. The AT overlaps it for roughly one hundred miles.

Shelter-
A permanent structure installed on a trail for the use of those travelling on it. Typically three-sided wood cabins with a roof. Common on eastern trails like the AT. They are first-come, first-served, and despite the entitlement mentioned by the drunken old man in the "Hero of Kent", there are no rules dictating any preference for occupation by a thru-hiker.

The Barefoot Sisters-
Hikers Lucy and Susan Letcher, known as Isis and Jackrabbit and collectively the Barefoot Sisters. They wrote two excellent books detailing their hikes on the AT, "The Barefoot Sisters Southbound" and "The Barefoot Sisters Northbound".

They are actual sisters. I think I would have married Isis had I not broken my leg, though that's pure speculation on my part.

The Whites-
The mountain range in New Hampshire that the AT travels through. The AMC (Appalachian Mountain Club) maintains this section and has several "Huts" that are rustic hotels. These and

other facilities are not 100% free, so some hikers bemoan the costs associated with hiking through some of the most spectacular land in the country. The people that work in the Huts are often college aged kids and are known as "Croo".

Base Camp-
When you leave your car or civilization behind much like a backpacker or canoeist might, but instead of breaking camp each day you set up a "base" camp and explore the surrounding area but return to the same spot at night.

Stealth Camp-
To use something other than a designated camp site. Leave no trace guidelines and park rules are followed.

Some assholes use this term to describe camping in illegal or alternate spots to avoid being charged a fee. As in, "I stealth camped just past the AMC caretaker so I didn't have to pay the $5." This is a form of bad medicine, and reading the final advice of Coyote Thunder Owl is suggested.

Shuttle-
Refers to getting a ride to or from the trail. A shuttle is often a paid service similar to a taxi ride. Although a trail angel may offer a ride as well. Different from hitchhiking in that it is slang for the service provided.

Taint-
The area between your genitals and your rectum.
(Hope you're not eating dinner.)

Long Distance Hiking and Trail Slang:

Northbounders (NOBO)-
Generally related to the AT but describes any hiker traveling from south to north, or northbound. On the AT, those that go NOBO also use the abbreviation GAME (Georgia to Maine GA-ME) to denote a successful hike.

Southbounders (SOBO)-
The opposite of NOBO, that's not hard now is it? These folks also use MEGA (Maine to Georgia) to abbreviate a successful hike. Occasionally SOBO's will be teased about going "the wrong way" as the vast majority of AT thru-hikes are NOBO.

Slack Pack-
To carry a less than full load, or only enough for a day hike while on a longer hike. Basically taking a "day hiking" break in the course of a long hike.

Day hiker-
As the name implies, someone out for the day with no intention to spend the night.

Flip-Flop-
A typical hike is done end to end style, but sometimes by choice, sometimes by need, a hiker will start at one end of the trail and then at some point "flip". This involves jumping to the other end of the trail and then turning around to the point you "flipped" from. One may also say they are thinking of "Flipping", or having already done so say they "flipped". Once the hike resumes, the spot you flipped from becomes your "end" of the trail.

Example: Mountain Laurel started the AT in Georgia, but slow pace and weather concerns led her to "flip" up to Maine from Delaware Water Gap. She started NOBO, traveled to Maine and finished her hike heading SOBO at DWG.

Katahdin is "closed" to hikers for a good portion of the late fall and early spring due to weather conditions. It is for this reason, and the possibility that one may hike 99.9% of the way only to be turned back and unable to finish the trail that many flip-flop. Maine to Vermont can be a very unpleasant place to be after September, so come late July/August, hikers not on track to finish the trail must choose if they will flip-flop.

This is primarily a NOBO choice, SOBO hikers have typically cleared the most dangerous parts of the trail by winter. Every year several people die in the Whites, it is not an area or choice to be taken lightly. Some hikers take being forced to flip-flop as a failure because they were forced to vary their plan of a "continuous" hike.

Thru-Hiker-
Quite simply, someone who completes a trail from start to finish in a continuous trip. Do not discuss the definition of this term on-line.

Section Hiker-
Refers to a hiker out for a portion of a long distance trail. It is also used to describe someone actively pursuing eventual completion of a long trail by hiking a portion (section) of that trail over several seasons.

Hiker Midnight-
About an hour after dark, or roughly 9:00pm. Most long distance hikers tend to fall into sync with the sun. Staying up late at home often means true midnight, hiker midnight is slang for staying up late on the trail.

Zero- (taking a zero)-
A "zero" is a day in which no miles are hiked. A rest day.

Yo-Yo-
Upon completing a long distance hiking trail the hiker then turns around and hikes it again in the opposite direction.

Trail Legs-
A term for the level of fitness reached after a long distance hiker spends three to eight weeks on the trail hiking. Essentially a point of "peak condition" is reached after hiking every day.

Mail Drops-
A form of resupply on a hike. A box, prepared by the hiker or a trusted friend is packed up prior to the trip and mailed to a local post office for pickup by the hiker via the post office general delivery system.

Drop Box-
The actual box used in a mail drop, as in "I need to hit the post office to pick up my drop box."

Consumer Commodity ORM-D-
A postal code that regulates the shipment of several backpacking items, most importantly, canister or solid stove fuel. These items are not allowed to be shipped via air, and must travel via ground transport.

Trail Angel-
Anyone (hiker or not) who goes out of their way to provide food or assistance to a hiker.

Trail Magic-
Generally used to describe when an unexpected gift or kindness is received by a hiker, whether another human is present or not.

Frequently it refers to a cache of food and drink left on the trail by a trail angel, something like a cooler of food and drinks with a note for a hiker to help themselves. As in, "Did you see the trail magic sitting near the last road crossing?"

Depending on your beliefs and experience, trail magic can take on a supernatural feel as the magic received begins to arrive just when needed or in exceedingly unusual ways. These extraordinary circumstances can be relatively common.

Yogi (Yogi'd)-

Like that cartoon picnic basket stealing bear we all know, to Yogi something is the art practiced by a long distance hiker to encourage, promote, or downright trick another passerby into giving up food, a ride, or assistance. Essentially it's a way for a hiker to encourage a stranger to become a trail angel. The degree to which the pressure (or art) is applied varies from hiker to hiker.

Despite the author's comments, it is a generally accepted practice and typically harmless activity.

Hiker Feed-

When a trail angel or organization sets up a place and invites hikers for a meal. Generally this is a fairly large picnic type event at a park near the trail or hosted by a local church or other group at their facility. Much more organized than a simple handout.

WhiteBlaze- www.whiteblaze.net
A website for discussion of hiking on the AT and other trails.

Blazes-
Manmade markers to indicate the route of an established trail.
White blazes- typical of the main route on the AT and LT.
Blue blazes- marking side trails on the AT.

The Trail Show- www.thetrailshow.com
A long distance hiking podcast focused primarily on beer. Though there is some hiking talk too.

TrailGroove- www.trailgroove.com
An online magazine catering to people with a pulse who like the outdoors.

Packed it out-
Refers to a backpacker picking up trash or any item that they feel should not have been left in the woods. A good deed.

No Rain, No Pain, No Maine-
A bit of a saying, a bit of a mantra during tough times. AT hikers use this to remind themselves that the journey is not always pleasant. It is often joined with: No downs, only ups, no water, only rocks, 'nother hole, need new socks.

Smell the Roses-
Refers to taking one's time while hiking to soak in and absorb the surroundings. Meant to be a gentle reminder to enjoy your hike, much like the often said, "It's about the smiles, not the miles."

Also used in a derogatory term between fellow hikers when one fails to enjoy a section or goes too quickly. Hikers often refer to speed hikers as "failing to smell the roses" in their rush. This is another one of those things best not discussed online.

Native American Terminology:

Depending on what tribe, and even what member of that tribe you might ask, you may receive a different answer. This book speaks for no person, nor as any authority, however, these definitions will serve in relation to the context of this book.

Keep in mind; what you read are my words only. There is no "Indian Bible", reference book, or single holy text. There is only the Earth and the universe it sits in. And I am only a human who shares my interpretation and definition. I'm a white fella who grew up in the burbs. I do not apologize for this, for the Earth belongs to all races, and speaks but one language.

Please remember what I believe to be the greatest appeal to any Native American philosophy: There are no correct answers, rigid definitions or absolute truths. Even if I were to consult some council of elders, great medicine men and women of each living tribe; each would give us a different answer. As mentioned in the book, if you want the truth, you can only find it on your own.

If you ask a traditional believing Sioux:
Who, exactly, is the Great Spirit or who is God?
They will honestly respond that they do not know.
Ed McGaa

Wakan Tanka-
Great Spirit, or more accurately, the Great Mystery.

Medicine-
A concept encompassing not only the personal power and energy of an individual being, but the flow of this energy (or spirit) from being to being.
Sometimes Medicine is referred to as "power". Or occasionally to describe the gifts of a particular being or spirit. The Spirit of the North is often associated with wisdom, and this is considered part the North's medicine, or power.

Or sometimes a person may be said to have a particular gift, such as strong Bear Medicine. Referring to their demonstration of being thoughtful and introspective, a gift often associated with Bear.

The Spirit That Moves Through All Things-
Definitions vary. But this is essentially the action of the medicine flowing, a sort of collective spirit describing the flow and connection of all things. It is a concept that in some form seems to exist not just in every religion or spiritual practice, but in science as well.

It does not imply or require a Higher Power or "Divine Hand" to guide it and exists outside of such a being if it were to exist. Although amongst those that do believe in some form of higher power, this spirit is said to be the spark of divinity found in each being.

Coyote-
The Trickster, Imitator, Sinkalip, and dozens of names.

A powerful figure in Native American mythology having many stories focused on his exploits. Generally considered a teacher, some tribes celebrate Coyote, some see him as an enemy. Entire books are written on Coyote, so an easy definition will not be found here. Perhaps if you meet him, you can decide for yourself.

Mitakuye Oyasin- (Me-tah Coo Yeh O Ya Seen)
We are all related, we are relations (family), we are all one. Sioux spelling, but a fairly universal concept, sometimes blended with the concept of the spirit that moves through all things, or as the fundamental concept that governs that movement.

Hoye wa yelo-(Ho-yeh Wah Yeh-low)
I am sending a voice... (Sioux spelling) Sometimes used to begin a story, address a crowd in ceremony, or to begin or end a prayer or ceremony. A formal address used when beseeching the Directions.

The Medicine Wheel and the Seven Directions-

East, South, West, North, Above (the sky, heavens, moon, sun), Below (The Earth), and Center (refers both to the great spirit and to the sacred center of all things, including us)

Generally the directions are considered parts of the whole, much as you may refer to a hand or foot separately from the body. Just as your hand is good for grabbing, your head good for thinking, the directions are generally treated in much the same manner. Spoken of separately with separate powers, but still part of Wakan Tanka. These are sometimes thought of as the "observable" parts of the Great Mystery. This concept continues to various animals and their Medicine. (And again, this is just my interpretation.)

The Wheel itself also contains many teachings, lessons, and further associations with elements, seasons, and other things beyond the scope of this glossary.

Geographical location plays a strong influence on what animals are used by each tribe, and in what location. The west coast tribes for example use Salmon in place of Buffalo.

Many tribes use only the four cardinal directions.

The Clan Chiefs-
East- Eagle
South- Coyote (Sinkalip)
West- Bear
North- Buffalo

The Clans-
Standing Ones-Trees and Plants
Winged Ones- All those that fly
Finned Ones- All those who dwell in the water
Crawling/Creeping Ones- Reptiles, Insects, Arachnid's, Etc.
Stone Clan- self explanatory
Four Legged- all the animals
Two Legged- the humans.

The "Naming Day" story (in Sinkalip)-

Also called "Coyote Keeps His Name" by some tribes and many variations exist. A common story in Native American mythology briefly summarized by Coyote Thunder Owl in Sinkalip. Coyote's name is considered an insult by some, as are trickster and imitator. For this reason, nobody, including Coyote, wanted his name. Coyote plots to gain a better name on naming day but fails.

Medicine Story-

A tale told to pass on a lesson, not intended to be taken literally or be entirely factual. A fable basically, but most assign more "weight" to them than a simple story. Medicine Stories are the closest thing many tribes have to a "holy" book and serve as an oral history. Many believed that some of the more powerful stories could impart medicine directly to those who heard them.

There are several such stories in this book and it is said that a good medicine story is always "true" regardless of the content. Often the stories are funny and entertaining, often even more so when the message is most powerful.

The Valley of the First People Story- (Told in Sinkalip)-

This is an "original" story, not told before or as a variation of an existing myth and follows the events after the Naming Day story.

Point being- don't go asking a Native American to tell you this tale or get angry at anyone but the author if you didn't like it. For what it's worth, I'm not the author, I don't know who is. I just pressed the keys, so don't get mad at me either.

Iktomi-

Spider, also a trickster and frequent companion to Coyote. They often refer to each other as "Cousin". In some tribes Iktomi serves the same role as Coyote.

In others Kokopelli is occasionally used as well, although this spirit is considered separate in many southwest tribes. In some tribes the Kokopelli tales are told with Coyote or Spider in place of Kokopelli.

Dropped their robes-

Refers to an individual voluntarily leaving their body, causing physical death. Or simply meaning; to die. In some nations older members would go off on a final journey when they felt their time on this earth had ended.

In times of need, it also refers to the sacrifice of a life for some greater purpose.

On the Trail of Tears it was often said that the Elders of the tribe would drop their robes; expending the last of their medicine to prevent the death of a child on a very cold evening or to give them strength to complete the march.

"Don't run away with a false idee, friend Cap, don't run away with a false idee. These things are only skin-deep, and all depend on edication and nat'ral gifts. Look around you at mankind, and tell me why you see a red warrior here, a black one there, and white armies in another place? All this, and a great deal more of the same kind that I could point out, has been ordered for some special purpose; and it is not for us to fly in the face of facts and deny their truth. No, no; each color has its gifts, and its laws, and its traditions; and one is not to condemn another because he does not exactly comprehend it."

"You must have read a great deal, Pathfinder, to see things so clear as this," returned Cap, not a little mystified by his companion's simple creed. "It's all as plain as day to me now, though I must say I never fell in with these opinions before. What denomination do you belong to, my friend?"

"Anan?"

"What sect do you hold out for? What particular church do you fetch up in?"

"Look about you, and judge for yourself. I'm in church now; I eat in church, drink in church, sleep in church. The 'arth is the temple of the Lord, and I wait on Him hourly, daily, without ceasing, I humbly hope."

James Fennimore Cooper- "Pathfinder"

Above:

Sometimes-

In the morning you awaken, a bit groggy from short rest. You look around for you campmate, only to find that your Ol' Pal Bill is gone. Sometime betwixt the late hour you lay your head down and the dawn he must have slipped away. If he was there at all, you wonder. But there lays the fire, burned down as promised. So you pack up and prepare to depart, to put this strange encounter behind you and move on.

But before you go, you stoop to inspect the fire. It is burned down neat and clean as promised, he did tell you that he takes such things seriously. A soft spot of white ash, like a pile of spider silk, appears to be all that is left behind.

You kneel down and hold a hand over. Cold out. You suck in a breath and blow away the ash to test the skill of the one who left it. As fine as flower pollen it gives way and scatters in the wind. In the bottom you find a faint glow.

A tiny ember, a dying coal, a faint spark. Another few minutes it would likely have been gone, a gentle breath prolonging its life as you ponder it. If you had slept a bit later, lingered longer, not bothered to verify that a promise was kept; it would be lost.

As it always seems to go with this sort of thing, if things had not worked out just so, just perfectly, you would have missed it. But somehow, you didn't. It appears something is left over of Just Bill from the evening after all.

One small spark of fire medicine has been left behind from the evening's tales for you. It isn't much truth be told, little worth the loss of sleep it took to earn it. This gift is no freebie either, it will take some effort on your part, but the potential is there. You realize you could take it up, rekindle it with gentle care. Feed it with the wind of your breath, fuel it with branches of earth, ignite your soul, build a campfire of your own.

A campfire and a liar and a promise.

You chuckle softly to yourself. Just when you thought you knew the truth, once again; Just Bill has lied to you.

A hike may end...but once you've set foot on it, the trail never does.

"Sometimes"

As performed by Sai Vedder and Pearl Jam

Large fingers pushing paint
You're god and you've got big hands
The colors blend...
The challenges you give man
Seek my part... devote myself
My small self... like a book amongst the many on a shelf

Sometimes I know,
Sometimes I rise
Sometimes I fall,
Sometimes I don't
Sometimes I cringe,
Sometimes I live
Sometimes I walk,
Sometimes I kneel
Sometimes I speak of nothing at all
Sometimes I reach to myself, dear god

Center:

My Home-

It has been said that astronomy is a humbling and character-building experience. There is perhaps no better demonstration of the folly of human conceits than this distant image of our tiny world. To me, it underscores our responsibility to deal more kindly with one another, and to preserve and cherish the pale blue dot, the only home we've ever known.

Carl Sagan, "Pale Blue Dot"

If you were to take this book seriously, and venture out into the outdoors, please know that you will be more than a simple traveler, you will be a guest in my home. The outdoors is more than just a place you will go for recreation, or escape from your urban lives. I would like to formally invite you to my home. Like any invited guest, I hope you will observe some basic courtesies while traveling my halls.

Imagine I am hosting a party at your house, and I invite an unlimited number of guests. Would they use your washroom and tuck the used waste papers into the corner? Would they finish their drinks and discard the cups into your hearth? Would they toss uneaten food into your bedroom? Wash their clothing in your kitchen sink? I think not, such behavior is unacceptable when entering someone's house, such guests would not be welcome, and the simple shame if caught in these behaviors would be enough to prevent many of them in the first place.

So too must you behave when in my house, such simple, civilized actions are no less welcome in the uncivilized lands where you will be a guest. However you will find the door always open, few if any other guests exist to police your behavior, so you must supervise yourselves.

In polite society most two-legged practice some form of the golden rule, "Treat others as you wish to be treated." In my home there are no rules, and no one to enforce them even if they existed. This freedom is why you came to visit, and why you choose to stay. Though no rules exist, there is a law. This law is a Truth; it cannot be taught, nor adequately written. A rule can be broken, a Truth, cannot. This law is universal, and like any Truth on this Earth, it is easy to say, hard to understand, and harder to live.

In your visits you may hear of trail magic, you may experience these events personally. For those of you not familiar, these are acts of kindness received by those who visit my home. Most commonly received from your fellow two legged, simple gifts of food, shelter, or hospitality as you travel. This magic is a simple gift, from one human to another. It restores your faith, your connection, and your bond with your fellow members of the human race. In my home these actions are termed, good medicine. Medicine being more than just a simple word, but rather a concept encompassing not only the personal power and energy of an individual, but also the flow of this energy from one being to another.

Mitakuye Oyasin; in the tongue of the Sioux, is a phrase similar in nature to the golden rule, but farther reaching, a Truth, a concept more full and all-encompassing than a simple rule. Translated it means: we are all related, we are all one. Like medicine these two words are more than just words, they are a philosophy, and a law that governs all actions and events. In my home there is not just good medicine, but also bad.

Any poor behavior, disrespectful actions to your host or his house will likely not be seen by any other human. No social pressure or stigma will prevent your actions, your invitation will not be revoked; no one will ask you to leave. This bad medicine however will follow you, and since this land is a place of medicine there you will begin to feel unwelcome. Roots will seem to tangle your feet, minor frustrations will become agonies, and you will experience the exact opposite of trail magic. You will have strained the goodwill and hospitality of your host, and subtle warnings will be issued.

Those of you with good hearts will come. You will respect the people that live there; you will treat others kindly and treat my home as you would treat your own. You may even find yourself correcting the mistakes of others who enter the outdoors. You will experience trail magic, good things will happen to you. You will feel the love of your fellow humans; you will benefit from their kindness and begin to see that you are all related. That all your actions have a relationship to the world around you; that you are not simply wishing to be treated well, that you are treated well.

You need not know anymore, you need not attribute any great spiritual meaning, join a religious group, worship or praise some higher power, or otherwise accept any belief in anything but the Truth. Mitakuye Oyasin. When you enter my home, you must accept the law of the land, nothing more, nothing less. You must simply understand the law, those who do not will always be welcome, but will quickly lose their taste to visit. You need know nothing more to travel my halls in peace, to be an honored guest during every visit.

Some of you however, will experience more.

You will receive trail magic filled with good medicine that transcends coincidence. You will receive gifts; they will be just what you need, exactly when you need it. Experiences that will stretch the boundaries of common sense, push the realm of practicality. You will begin to receive help from outside your immediate relations of the two-legged clan. You will begin to meet the others who live in my home.

When the halls of my home begin to bend, not to your will, but in good will, you will learn the Truth. Soft earth cushions your feet, rain quenches your thirst, fire warms your camp, and the wind blows at your back. When your tears flow with thanks, your heart swells with joy, your soul fills with wonder, and your spirit flies freely across the land, you will understand the Truth.

When my father shines on your face, my mother cradles you in your sleep, you will begin to wonder. When you meet the other clans; the four legged, the winged, the finned, the plants, the insects, and the crawling ones. When you walk under the arms of the standing ones, climb on the backs of the stone clan, and when you see all the directions, you will begin to understand who all the people that dwell in my house are. When you form a relationship with all the residents of my home, then the true hospitality will begin to flow. When you begin to feel love for all the people who dwell there, for all your relations you will begin to feel that love returned.

If ever bad medicine flows your way, you need only look to yourself. Many guests bring heavy burdens to my home; no one stands to take your coat at the door. When you are ready to part with your baggage you will find ample room, though the parting may be difficult. Some rooms in my home are filled with mirrors, reflecting your faults, making you feel unwelcome. But these hardships are merely another form of hospitality, my home educating you to its Law, helping you to overcome your troubles.

The land is a great teacher to those with the courage to learn its lessons. When you become a model guest, you will find no limits to the hospitality received.

Many of you will enter my home; you will sit at my hearth, drink, eat, and enjoy the company and fellowship of all who live there. You will gain respect and love for these people, you will become not merely equals, but you will see that you are all the same. A part of the whole.

One day you will arrive at my home. You will approach the door to knock and gain entry. Your hand will stall as you read the words written on the door, seen fully for the first time. Your hand will fall to your side.

Mitakuye Oyasin.

You will know my home for what it truly is. We are more than just related, we are one. My home is all the people that live there, all the people who live there are my home. My home is alive. You are related to my home, you are my home.

Your hand will reach once more for the door, without knocking you will push it open and enter; after all, you are no longer a guest.

Welcome home.

Walk in peace,

Coyote Thunder Owl